Unfatherless: Finding The Way Home

Sean D Alcorn

Published by S.D. Alcorn, 2024.

Table of Contents

Prologue 1
You're Not Special 3
Good Enough? Do Better 11
More Than Words Can Say 21
Hand-Me-Downs 31
How Do I Get There? 41
A Hero(?) Is Born 51
Balancing The Books 63
I Tried 75
He Didn't Have To Be 83
Something To Be Proud Of 95
A Place In The Sun 103
That Ain't No Way To Go 111
Not That Cliché About Onions 119
Happily Maybe Sometimes After 129
Knock Knock. Who's There? I AM. 137

UNFATHERLESS: FINDING THE WAY HOME
First edition. June 19, 2024.
Copyright © 2024 Sean D. Alcorn.
ISBN: 978-1068877803
Written by Sean D. Alcorn.

ALL RIGHTS RESERVED No part of this publication may be reproduced, stored in a retrieval system, or transmitted in any form by any means—electronic, mechanical, photocopying, recording, or otherwise—without prior written consent.

While every precaution has been taken in the preparation of this book, the publisher assumes no responsibility for errors or omissions, or for damages resulting from the use of the information contained herein.

All Scripture quotations, unless otherwise indicated, are taken from the Holy Bible, New International Version®, NIV®. Copyright ©1973, 1978, 1984, 2011 by Biblica, Inc.™ Used by permission of Zondervan. All rights reserved worldwide. www.zondervan.com The "NIV" and "New International Version" are trademarks registered in the United States Patent and Trademark Office by Biblica, Inc.™

Scripture quotations marked (NLT) are taken from the *Holy Bible*, New Living Translation, copyright ©1996, 2004, 2015 by Tyndale House Foundation. Used by permission of Tyndale House Publishers, Carol Stream, Illinois 60188. All rights reserved.

*"A father to the fatherless, a defender of widows,
is God in His holy dwelling.
God sets the lonely in families,
He leads out the prisoners with singing..."*
(Psalm 68:5-6)

Author's Note

Memory can be a tricky thing. Before we can recall anything, we need to commit it to memory, which is sometimes done consciously and sometimes not. When we do file away events which have occurred and the thoughts and feelings we associate with those events, can any one of us say that those files are 100% accurate and complete? The events in my story are all real, as I remember them and as I experienced them from my perspective. The one exception is the prologue, where although the core event is real, I've imagined the more intricate details which I could not possibly know.

Throughout, I state observations about human nature and the human mind as if they are fact. Feel free to disagree with any of these statements. They are simply the outcome of some education, some experience, and others' stories I've heard all thrown into a blender in my brain and poured back out through my fingertips.

Though I've tried not to vilify anyone within these pages, and believe I have succeeded, most names have been changed out of simple respect for privacy. Those names which have not been changed are those of people who deserve credit for the positive roles they have played.

Special thanks go to my beta readers; those who took the time with my initial manuscript to tell me what needed improvement. If anything you read in this book does not make sense, it is most likely because I stubbornly refused to make a suggested change. In no particular order, thank you Vanessa Reddecopp, Pamela Doerksen, Chris Kushman, and Kellin Friesen.

Most of all, thank you to my incredible wife, Lori. Without you, there would be no me, let alone this book. A thousand troops of Koopas couldn't keep me from you.

Prologue

It was a cool summer's eve as the man drove toward the house where he used to live. He expected that his arrival would be a surprise, having not been invited so much as compelled to go there. The unknown kept him at a level of unease which couldn't quite be described as anxiety, but more of a curious hope tempered by low expectations. With the car radio off and the windows down, a whispering breeze acted as a calming distraction from the plethora of possible scenarios he might encounter. Had he allowed his imagination to surmise anything close to what actually transpired during this visit, fear of the life-altering change which resulted may have motivated him to turn his car around.

Instead of being deterred by doubt, he pressed on in the way anyone might drive home from work on their regular route; with that "auto-pilot" navigation which comes so naturally from familiar old routines. It was only once he parked across the street from the three bedroom bungalow and killed the engine that he paused to consider what might come next. So many little things could have altered the timing and therefore the timeline. Accepting the offer of overtime before leaving work, choosing a different fast food drive-thru with a longer or shorter line, slowing for that one yellow light instead of zipping through before it turned red. Whether by whim or by destiny, these choices had already been made, and those to soon follow would be no different.

Before any coherent thought could form, let alone develop into decision, the sight of another man through the picture window of his former home triggered another form of "auto-pilot". Any preconceived notion that he may have had about how this evening would unfold was immediately overrun by simple reaction to the situation at hand.

Gordon strode to the front door at a gait as natural as he could manage under this unfamiliar circumstance. Having been divorced from his wife for only a short time, he tried to quell the destructive whispers in his mind telling him that he might have been replaced so soon, so easily. Surely there were other possible reasons for this other man's presence in *his* home, where *his* three young children would now be sleeping. Yet, assuming the worst possible scenario had become a characteristic of his already broken heart. With his pulse steadily increasing toward a rapid-fire pace, he mounted the steps to the front door. While knocking, he became lost in the wonder of exactly when and how he had forfeited the right to simply walk inside.

After what may have been a time, times, or half a time, his ex-wife's screams for help as she ran to the neighbour's house startled Gordon out of a black cloud of confusion to one of rage. At least, he initially correlated the rage he was feeling with the dark red colour filling his line of sight. As mere seconds passed, each of which felt like an eternity, the realization dawned on him that the red was not a cloud, but a pool. The body of the man who had been in his home was seeping, no, pouring blood on to the front walkway. As Gordon's field of vision slowly cleared and widened, he saw that he was somehow now on the inside of the doorway looking out at this scene. Wanting to see anything other than the horror which had somehow appeared before him, he looked straight down, and then wondered how his hunting rifle had ended up in his hands.

Gordon's hope and the whisper of the evening breeze were simultaneously replaced with despair and the sound of wailing sirens.

You're Not Special

"An abnormal reaction to an abnormal situation is normal behaviour." – Viktor Frankl, Man's Search for Meaning

I was barely five years old, the youngest of Gordon's three boys, when he shot a man nine times, killing him before any help could arrive. To this day, I still don't know whether my mother was his second intended target who happened to escape, or if she made it safely to our neighbour's house out of some form of grace he exercised. Perhaps he simply ran out of ammunition. Regardless, his seemingly senseless murder of one person was enough to alter the trajectory of my development. The path forged by Gordon is likely different than that which was the catalyst of your story, but the wake left behind may sound familiar. Even my own two brothers, growing up in the same home in the aftermath of the same situation, each have stories strikingly different from mine. However, many of our symptomatic struggles stem from similar roots.

Without the benefit of any formal teaching or guidance on how to deal with the psychological, emotional, and spiritual fallout, the coping mechanisms and unhealthy behaviours we develop in reaction to traumatic experiences are actually quite normal. That is, normal in the sense that those of us who have felt abandoned and unloved hold them in common. They are not a normal part of our intended growth and development as children of God. After all, He says: *"'For I know the plans I have for you', declares the Lord, 'plans to prosper you and not to harm you, plans to give you a hope and a future'"* (Jeremiah 29:11). Though those words were spoken in the context of God proclaiming to the nation of Israel that their captivity at the time would end, they are one of many examples of God's heart toward His children. Regardless of our own personal struggles, He desires the same thing for every one of us: hope, and a future, and so much more. In spite of the uniqueness of each of our situations, we've all been created equally. Sometimes in our own limited wisdom we don't see any benefit to being one of many. We often believe our suffering is unique and may even want to believe that nobody would understand. We want to feel special, and in absence of being treated as though we are special in a healthy, loving way we fill the gap by defining our uniqueness by our pain. We sometimes want to be as unique as a snowflake. Being a snowflake implies that there is no other like you, but when you apply heat to any snowflake, the reaction and the results are the same.

In my early years, I knew grass was green, the sky was blue, and that my father was a murderer. It was a taboo subject in my family (that is, my father, not the grass nor the sky), so how I knew I cannot say. Even the prologue to this book contains a dose of imagination wrapped around the core truth of the events of that night. Neuroscience tells us there is a link between psychological trauma and long-term memory deficits, which combined with my age at the time of the incident could explain the lack of personal recollection. Prior to corroborating the story through old newspaper articles and court documents later in my life, it was always just one of those facts that we so often accept without question. It may have been one of those conversations that adults have when they don't realize the children can overhear. Chances are it was one of my older brothers who told me, though I don't specifically remember either of them or anyone else doing so. At the time, the stain on the front walk which took months to turn from crimson to rust before finally fading away was evidence enough.

As I began to grow older and presumably more intelligent, I learned the scientific explanations of photosynthesis and of the refraction of the sun's light through Earth's atmosphere. The more important explanation of my father's choice to murder another human being was never covered in school, unless I somehow missed that elective. I wasn't taught to differentiate his actions from his feelings toward me, and so I took his absence personally. I was left to fill in the blanks of why a man would abandon his son, why it had to happen to me, and why I had to live a life that could turn out this way. It was the worst "Mad Libs" I've ever played.

As alone as I felt at the time, I've since heard countless stories of people expressing difficulty with their own self-worth and identity. Some come from a history of abuse, some come from families full of love and encouragement. Nobody deserves to be abused. If abuse is a part of your past, I am sorry that happened to you. I want you to know that it was not your fault, and that it was undeserved. I have no intent to compare any one person's suffering to another's. One thing I've learned is that a person does not need to experience trauma in order to question the reason for their existence and the pain that inevitably accompanies life. In spite of the unique details of each story, the commonality is that something went wrong, something that was undeserved or unfair. Whether your story includes a blatant, obvious injustice, or an internal psychological or emotional offense that others cannot easily see, I would wager that the majority of humanity would claim to have suffered to at least some degree at some point in life. For those of us whose suffering was in the absence of formal education about mental health and the development of healthy coping mechanisms, we were left to grope around in the shadows of our individual sufferings, taking hold of whatever seemingly stable solution we could find.

It is human nature to expect justice, and when our expectation of justice is challenged we tend to seek out restoration from our suffering. It is also human nature to call out to a higher power in times of even the smallest suffering. Anyone who has had trouble with their car battery in the dead of winter knows exactly what it's like to ask God for help, whether they believe He exists or not. We so naturally ask God "why?" when even the slightest of things goes against our expectations. It's as if we instinctually know that someone is not only listening, but might have the power and the desire to improve our situation. The innate need to know why our suffering exists leaves us with a need to seek out answers, comfort, and resolution. Sometimes the difference is in where we place our faith. If crying out to God while trying to start my car doesn't work, I'm going to call roadside assistance because I believe and trust they will come provide a jumpstart or a tow. There is nothing wrong with leaning on our own abilities and on the resources around us for such insignificant things.

When our suffering is greater, relying on our limited abilities and resources can lead to further suffering. If the question to God was *"why does he hit me?"*, *"why does she drink so much?"*, *"why aren't I as pretty as the other girls?"*, *"why am I always picked last for a team?"*, or anything else that we associate with our identity and self-worth, then placing our faith in worldly answers often lacks fulfillment. So often, leaning on our own knowledge and understanding leads only to methods to deal with the symptoms of our issue. It's great to eliminate symptoms, but that does not go far enough. Without dealing with the root cause, ridding ourselves of one negative thought or feeling can easily lead to seven others being allowed in.

Finding solace in imperfect "easy" relationships, in substances, in mind-numbing distractions or adrenaline highs may be a quick fix, but simply living for that next fix does not fix anything. Our impatience and avoidance can often be our downfall, whereas patience and perseverance through suffering can lead to restoration and healing. There is more to be done than to deal with our issues, we must move past them into a new way of living in order to truly be free of our past sufferings. We also need help from the One whose original plan was *"to prosper you"* and *"to give you hope"*, the One who wants to see us through. *"The Lord longs to be gracious to you; therefore he will rise up to show you compassion. For the Lord is a God of justice. Blessed are all who wait for him!"* (Isaiah 30:18).

As a five year old boy, I did not have any belief or trust that I might hear from God if I would just exercise some patience and persistence. Placing too much importance on the fact that my father was a murderer led me to believe that a number of different shadows were truth. Any questions I had couldn't be asked outside of the confines of my solitude. As the youngest of three boys, I was the annoyance to my older brothers who they were forced to watch over while our mother had to work two jobs to support us. They had their friends, and the tag-along baby brother was an unwanted responsibility. When our mother was home, she would never speak of our father even if asked about him, leading me to adopt the belief that it was a secret subject, a source of embarrassment and shame. Believing that lie disallowed me from reaching out to anyone, leaving me to my own devices.

Religion and spirituality were neither practiced nor pursued in our home. The extent of my exposure to these things as a child was to learn Jesus' name as a curse. I had one friend on the same block who I knew was dragged to church every Sunday, but all he said about it was that he wished he didn't have to go. Somehow in spite of the lack of any teaching or any example being set, I must have known or at least suspected that God does exist. I certainly wasn't crying out to nothingness, to a cold expansive void which houses countless stars.

My heart needed a jumpstart, and possibly even a tow. "Fate", "destiny", and "the universe" are impersonal concepts. They are each incapable of answering questions, offering comfort, or causing resolution. As so many do in times of anguish, I inferred that there must be meaning. If there is meaning, there must be intent. If there is intent, there must be an intender. In between assumption and truth, however, there is sometimes another type of cold, expansive void which we tend to fill with whatever fits; more assumptions, misunderstandings, belief in lies, and cheap or twisted copies of the fulfillment we desire. The shadow versions of what we desire cannot offer lasting fulfillment, and chasing after them is a sure way to veer off of the path that leads toward our true selves.

Sometimes it only takes a minor error in a flight plan, only a few degrees off course, for a plane to end up far from its intended destination after the proper amount of time in flight. In the same way, sometimes it only takes a whisper in the night to send echoes of dysfunction reverberating through our lives. One of the earliest questions I can remember asking is, *"didn't my dad care enough about me to not go to jail?"* Considering that he did what he did, the answer obvious to me at the time was that he must not have cared about me. In my young mind, he simply could have chosen to not commit a crime that would sentence me to life imprisoned by abandonment.

In Plato's *"Allegory of the Cave"*, he posits that our perception of the world is akin to that of people who have spent their life in darkness, chained up and facing a cavern wall. Behind them is a fire, casting dim light toward the wall they face. In between them and this fire, objects are moved from one side to the other, casting shadows within their sight. Unable to turn around to see the true objects, the prisoners assume these shadows to be the truth. They assign a meaning to them, and even name them. *"I'll call that one 'puppy'"*, for example. If ever they are released from their chains and encounter an actual puppy, imagine their aww! I mean, imagine their awe at the idea that reality is so much more than what their limited exposure has allowed them to believe. Plato goes on to surmise what the different reactions of these people might be upon their release. One may be fearful and unaccepting of the truth, considering it to be the lie, because undoing years of belief often takes more than one encounter. Another may become curious at the sight and begin moving toward the cave exit. This one will soon be faced with a choice once they encounter sunlight. Exponentially greater than the light cast by the fire, the sunlight will be painful at first. The temptation to turn around and hide back in the familiar darkness will be great. The brightness of the sun will be so overwhelming, they may need another person who has already experienced the warmth of the sun to encourage them onward, into freedom. Many of us have times in our lives when we need to choose our pain. The pain of change may seem to outweigh the pain of our current situation, but we often neglect to consider that the duration of the change-pain could be the shorter of the two. It may seem obvious that acclimating to sunlight is a temporary discomfort that is well worth the escape from a dungeon in a cave, but metaphorically speaking we often choose the chains.

    To describe this concept in another way, imagine growing up in a home cut off from the world where the only mirror is like one from a circus funhouse. Every time you see your face in the mirror, the reflection staring back at you is distorted in some way. With no access to any other point of reference, the obvious conclusion is that the mirror is showing your true face. Even if you hold another object to the mirror and compare it to the warped reflection, the revelation that the mirror is inaccurate is still not enough to show you your true face. You're essentially living a life chained in darkness. One day, you may not live there anymore. In the interim though, the only picture you have of yourself is false. If this goes on long enough, you may even refuse to believe what you're seeing if you ever encounter your true reflection. Years of belief build and reinforce a distrust of the true mirror, especially if it shows blemishes of which you were previously unaware. You have a choice to turn back to what you've always believed out of fear of the unknown, or fear of change. Conversely, you can experience the pain that comes with change and acclimation to the sun, the light, the truth. Through that pain, on the other side, you may find freedom.

    In my imprisonment, or life with the funhouse mirror if you prefer, crying out to God for answers seemed as fruitless as a tree that is cursed and withered. I had never set foot in a church nor opened a bible, I had no concept of prayer, and the only listening I had ever really done was to listen to instructions from grown-ups. Note that I didn't say following instructions, that's something completely different. My expectation of a relationship with God was that I asked the questions, and in an audible voice He would answer without delay. In the absence of such a response it didn't take long for me to assume that if God did care about people, I wasn't special enough to be one of them. Though I have no recollection of how, I somehow knew that He is referred to as a father, and so I boxed Him into the expectation I had developed of a father. Absent, uncaring, unloving, uncommunicative of whatever impossibly high standards He had which I could never satisfy. I thought that I was unique in my suffering, and that I had to come up with my own answers. Without any co-pilot or air traffic control tower to double check my flight plan, I set my course based upon my own conclusions, each of which were a few degrees off of the intended mark.

"I'm not good enough for anyone to care about."
"Even my brothers pick on me all the time, so I can't trust anybody."
"I'll never be a man because nobody is going to show me how."
"I have a murderer's blood in my veins, so I'll probably end up just like him."
"My own father didn't want to be around me, why would anyone else?"

The whispers that entered my mind as a child reverberated through my life for far too long. They stole my identity. They killed my self-worth. They destroyed my willingness to love, and to be loved. As time went on, new experiences added new voices to the cacophonous chorus narrating my story. Rather, my interpretation of those experiences amplified those whispered lies to a lion-like roar, making it easy and even natural for me to perpetuate my own pain. Echoes do fade over time, but without seeing and silencing the source, they can and likely will repeat. Even a five year old child ought to realize that clenching your eyes shut, sticking your fingers in your ears and shouting "LA-LA-LA" is only a temporary solution. The problem with drowning out the noise is that it also prevents us from hearing the soft, gentle voice of anyone who might be trying to help. We need to listen closely for the queues that will bring us closer to wholeness, sometimes retracing our steps to the origin of our wandering.

The metaphor we so often hear used when it comes to dealing with our past is that weeds need to be torn out by the roots, or they're just going to come back. It's a good and true metaphor, and don't get me wrong, I dislike weeds very much. On the other hand, I think that we can learn a lot from weeds. They don't care if we think they're ugly, or useless, or always in the way. It doesn't matter how unwanted they might be. We can cut them, burn them, poison them, and yes, even tear them out by the roots. Regardless of what we do to them, weeds always do what weeds do. They grow. They reach upward, toward the light. Your situation may seem to be as unique as any individual snowflake, but all a snowflake does is fall, then sit there, then melt. There is nothing special about falling down, staying where you land, and then falling apart. It may be tempting to take that easy route, to stay in the pain of your current situation out of fear of being unwanted, being cut, burned, or poisoned, or even having your roots torn out. The thing about roots is, they are often resilient enough to survive being transplanted to firmer, richer soil when done with the care of an expert.

It takes a special kind of spirit to not care if anyone thinks you're ugly, or useless, or always in the way, or unwanted. It takes a special kind of spirit to go through suffering in a way that produces perseverance, character, and hope for a future. It is a truly special story to hear when someone has the courage to choose the pain of change, and the resiliency to persevere through. We need courage and resilience because a soul, like a seed, is sometimes dead and buried before it sprouts, pushes through the dirt, and reaches upward toward the light of the sun. Rather, the light of the Son. I know; I've been there.

Good Enough? Do Better

"We cannot think of being acceptable to others until we have first proven acceptable to ourselves." – Malcolm X

Life is not like a box of chocolates. It's true that you may never know what you're going to get in life, but a box of chocolates has a label. An assorted box of chocolates has a legend, with pictures and descriptions of which chocolate is which. Mint? No, thank you. Mint belongs in my toothpaste, not my dessert. If I'm given a box of chocolates I'm not particularly fond of, nothing is forcing me to eat them. I could go to the store and buy the kind I want. I could choose the box that has a variety within, or a box of entirely the same kind. Maybe I'll get the two-bite brownies instead, even though they falsely advertise with the idea that they might last longer than one bite. I'm not boxed into the confines of what has been placed in front of me. Somehow, when Tom Hanks stated *"mama always said life is like a box of chocolates"* in the 1994 hit movie *Forrest Gump*, society latched on to the catchy phrase and deemed it profound. Perhaps it is an acceptable simile in some situations, but in others it fits about as well as the clothes I wore in high school fit my body today. Thank you, one-bite brownies, those clothes no longer fit. With all due respect to both Forrest Gump and his mama, I must disagree. Life is much more complicated, and that's *not* all I've got to say about that.

Questioning the wisdom of *Forrest Gump* may seem preposterous. Questioning the beliefs that take hold in our minds at an early age can seem equally, if not more preposterous. That is, if it even occurs to us to question those beliefs after they've been a part of our way of being for so long. The coping mechanisms we've developed are sometimes good enough to keep us moving along through life, but there is a difference between simply getting by and actually living life. Just because something is "good enough", that does not mean it is either good, or enough.

One of the best methods to assist in memorization is through repetition. Also, a really great way to help yourself remember things is through repetition. Behaviours, attitudes, and beliefs are no different. When we go through life reinforcing beliefs which originated in the dark cavern of our minds, we eventually accept our default behaviours as the right thing to do, regardless of how unhealthy they may be. These beliefs and behaviours may have served us well to protect us from some perceived possibility of pain, but looking at that risk through the funhouse mirror made our original, foundational assumptions inaccurate. Imagine if the pilot in the earlier example of a plane that is just a couple of degrees off course has a successful take-off, a smooth flight, and a perfect landing. If you were a passenger on that plane and ended up in a completely different destination than intended, would you accept his explanation that it's "good enough"? You would probably not think it is good at all, and likely would not agree that the airline had done enough. If the pilot had double-checked his instruments, he may have been on course. And yes, I'm assuming the pilot in this example was a man because after all, he didn't ask for directions. When we find ourselves somewhere that doesn't seem right, we may need to retrace our path to the point from which we set upon the wrong course. We may need to question whether what seemed right at the time was actually wrong, or vice versa.

It can be difficult to know if something is wrong without knowing what "right" looks like. Some people even assert that the entire concept of "right and wrong" existing is wrong. I'm not sure how that concept can be wrong in an ideology where wrong doesn't exist. One thing I am sure of is that regardless of what you call it, we all want something better. A better job, house, or car. Better relationships. Better behaved children, better parents. A better opportunity to help people. Better weather. A better pilot. A better box of chocolates. Our motives may differ, and further divergence comes in our various definitions of "better". Yet we all strive for something, and our yearnings are spurred on by examples in our lives of what we view as "right", or "better", or "good". There is nothing wrong with wanting to improve our lives or our situations, but there seems to always be a desire for more. If we achieve what we've been coveting, it doesn't take long before something "better" presents itself, changing our perspective of what we now have to one of dissatisfaction. Simply succumbing to the thought that it would be better to have something we don't or to be somebody we are not ruins our ability to be content with what we have or who we are. This can spur us on in a healthy manner to achieve a goal, but can also be a trigger toward destructive patterns.

On the block where I continued to live for two years after our home became a crime scene, there lived another boy my age. Having met at an age where venturing too far from home without a grown-up was forbidden, and being the only two boys our age on the same block, Ryan and I became friends out of circumstance. Ryan was different from me in a few ways. He was more athletic, he was the oldest of two children rather than the youngest of three, his parents had better jobs which afforded him an allowance and nicer, better things. Most of all, he had a father who was still married to his mother. A father who still lived with him. A father who did all of the "right" things, such as taking him to the movies, or to the park to play ball. A father who taught him how to ride a bike. A father who, as embarrassing as it may have been to a growing boy, would hug Ryan and tell him that he loved him. A father.

Through the incredible powers of deduction and reasoning that I had developed by the age of six, I made the logical assumption that if I were more like Ryan, and did the "right" things, I would deserve the acceptance and love of a father. He obviously hadn't done whatever it was that I had done wrong to make my father abandon me. From my perspective, he was "better", and "good". So, I did what I could to take advantage of every opportunity to be around him and mimic his behaviours. Of course, at that age there was no conscious thought, no moment in time when I made the intentional decision to try to pattern myself after another person. It was simply as if some part of me knew that he had something which I was missing. I had not yet come to understand that, being incarcerated, my father literally could not return. I had not yet developed the self-awareness to question my own behaviours or motives. Nor did I have experiences on which to rely, to guide me to decide to be the individual who I was intended to be. I set out on a course which I thought would be better, because I had a desire for something someone else had. I didn't even think to double-check my course, or to ask for directions.

At first, it was easy to find ways to spend time with Ryan. Sometimes we would ride our bikes around the neighbourhood, often ending up in the nearby park with our toy guns. Back in those days, kids played with toy guns in public and nobody ever called the police. Rainy days might have been spent in either of our homes, though mostly his because it was better not to burden my older brothers with our presence. Also, he had better toys, and more of them. I was always willing to go along with whatever activity he proposed, because he obviously knew the right things to do in order to deserve a father. If I wanted anything, it was to deserve the same thing. Any desire I might have had to play with Hot Wheels instead of G.I. Joe action figures (they're not dolls!) on any given day was insignificant by comparison, so I wouldn't dare suggest anything contrary to Ryan's plans. It's not like he was demanding or controlling, I was just content to be allowed to spend time with him and soak up any of his father's wisdom or guidance which might overflow. I was especially pleased to be in his good graces when opportunities arose to be a guest on outings with his father, or to be invited for the occasional sleep-over where I could almost imagine that I was a part of a normal family.

Ryan and I even remained friends in spite of one event which tempted both of our mothers to prevent us from ever seeing one another again. I'm sure each one of them wanted to place blame on the child who was not hers after my mother allegedly found the two of us standing in the nearby intersection of a busy street, directing traffic. I have no recollection of this incident, but apparently she was drawn out by her curiosity of the ongoing blaring of car horns. It seems that one of us thought it would be fun to play traffic police, and why rely solely upon our imaginations when there was a perfectly good real-life road right there? I'm told by my mother that the only reason she stopped yelling at me over the incident was because the ringing phone interrupted her. Ryan's mom had called to yell at *her* for sending him home crying. That is, until my mother explained that Ryan had only reacted that way when she scolded us for trying to die. Somehow, after what was likely a lengthy grounding, Ryan and I were allowed to play together once again, though, on supervised probation for a time.

It wasn't long before school started. In spite of my older brothers' declarations that it was run by demons and witches with the sole purpose of tormenting children, I knew that I would get through as long as I had my best friend at my side to show me how to cope. I knew Ryan was my best friend, because he was my only friend. The fact that he had a father to teach him the things that would turn a boy into a man meant that all I had to do was follow his lead. I also knew that he would help me as best he could, because after all the time we had spent together, I must also be his best friend. He even relied on me for something now; I had the older brothers who were forced to shoulder the responsibility of walking us to and from school every morning and afternoon, thus ensuring we would at least spend that time together. The in-between had no such guarantee, but I assumed that as long as I continued to follow the leader, there would be no reason for anything to change. The idea that Ryan might leave me behind while pursuing his own interests never crossed my mind. How could he, if I would just adopt the same interests?

Ryan was a good friend. He wasn't manipulative, nor a bully. If anything, he might have subconsciously enjoyed having a sidekick, but I was the one with the problem. Living in a home of denial is not conducive to learning how to express thoughts, opinions, or feelings. In hindsight, I can understand my mother's desire for whatever free time she had to not be occupied with reminders of what her ex-husband had done. It makes sense now that she didn't model empathy through those years, and neither facilitated nor even entertained discussion about the impact of that traumatic event. Through no fault of her own, she simply did not have the tools. So, at the time, I hadn't learned the empathy required for insight to her point of view. What I did learn was to put on a display so that nobody would see that anything was wrong. I learned to never argue. I learned to never bring up an idea that would require effort out of someone else for my benefit. I learned that negative feelings were something to just get over, by yourself, because nobody wants to hear about them.

To be clear, I love my mother and know that she loves me. The unhealthy coping mechanisms I learned were not anything that she actively or intentionally taught; they were constructs of my own mind, molded from my own observations and assumptions. There were times when I would come home from school and break down crying because of some bully, and she was there for me. There were good times, such as when I would "help" her bake a cake by licking the bowl clean of the batter (and the seeds of a one-bite brownie addiction were sown). She did what she could with the circumstances which were thrust upon her. Regardless of the good times, I learned that it was "good enough" to just get through each day without being hurt, without being betrayed, and without being abandoned.

A codependent person, though historically defined as one who remains in an unhealthy relationship because they feel responsible for taking care of a person with a problem, can actually be defined more broadly. When the term was first used, it typically applied to an enabler who would allow and even perpetuate others' behaviours such as addiction, abuse, manipulation, or narcissism just to name a few. The codependent person sets aside their own needs and desires, and sometimes their own well-being in favour of maintaining the relationship, or some semblance of peace within the relationship. The concept of codependence has evolved and become more widely applied over time, to refer more to the behaviour of the codependent person and to focus less on the other person in the relationship. It's true that a codependent person is much more likely to overlook, accept, or even cover for shortfalls in others in order to maintain the relationship. However, the signature of the codependent is more of a relationship addiction, regardless of the behaviours of the other person. They may attach themselves to somebody who is generally healthy. Being codependent is like being prone to addiction; exposure to alcohol or pain medications are likely to result in substance abuse, but it's also just as possible to be addicted to something that is good for you, like coffee. Regardless of what my wife might tell you, coffee is indeed good for you. A codependent person who is exposed to a manipulative or needy individual is likely to assume responsibility which is not theirs, with the goal of maintaining the relationship. Being exposed to a person who is genuinely nice and encouraging can also draw a codependent person into an unhealthy or even obsessive attachment, out of a desire or need for the acceptance found in this relationship. Ryan was genuinely nice and encouraging toward me, so I made every effort to remain attached to this relationship where I never expected to be hurt, betrayed, or abandoned.

The days at school were filled with opportunities for both Ryan and me to make new friends. This was not an easy task for me. The only friend I had was the one upon whom I had been forced due to circumstance, and so my method of making new friends was to ensure that I was around him as much as possible, especially when other kids might try to replace me as his best friend. The only relational tools I had were to go along with the crowd so as to not lose even the slightest degree of acceptance I might have earned. I had learned from my older brothers that I could be very useful in practicing wrestling moves, but I wasn't about to volunteer in that role for others. I don't care how fake wrestling might be, a figure-four leg-lock hurts. The kids at school seemed to place value on physical matters more so than mental acuity. My natural ability to achieve high test scores, combined with my supernatural ability to never catch a ball that was thrown my way quickly determined my lack of value in this social structure. If only I had a father to teach me to be more like Ryan, whose popularity grew as time went on, I might have been seen as worthy of friendship. Friends were plentiful for him, and though he never intentionally left me out, it became more and more difficult for him to intentionally include me. I wasn't fast enough on a bike to keep up with the crowd. I wasn't talented enough at football or hockey to contribute to a winning team. I wasn't good enough to be included, to be accepted. Saying anything to Ryan about this would have been a display of emotion, which I had learned was wrong. So, I did what I believed to be right. I kept my mouth shut, I acted as if everything was fine, and I was happy to spend any time with my best friend that I was able.

Though he never treated me as such, in absence of being afforded a seat at the table I became like a dog patiently waiting for any scraps which might fall to the floor. On the outside, I was the friend who always seemed to just happen to be available when Ryan didn't have something better to do. He never knew that in his absence, my brothers were my only social circle. I refrained from showing any of my true self, and instead gave time and energy to being accepted in what I thought was the only way I would be; by making others happy.

Being accepted for what you can give is acceptance not of you, but of what you can give. Being accepted for what you can give may seem good enough, but again, it is neither "good" nor "enough". It's a conditional acceptance, and it teaches us that we must always have something to give in order to be of any value in relationships, thus perpetuating the problem. There is nothing wrong with giving, unless of course you're trying to give me mint flavored chocolates or a figure-four leg-lock. There is such a thing as giving too much, or giving too freely. You can only give what you have received, and so if your identity and self-worth are tied to this conditional acceptance, who are you when you run out of anything to give? Without an answer to that question, we become chameleons. We do our best to blend into whatever relationship offers us some modicum of belonging, willing to give whatever is asked of us. This codependent behaviour not only strikes the heel of our own well-being, but can, and often ends up pushing us past lines of morality and values which we might have previously held. We end up far from our intended destination, all because of a slight error in the initial course. It's never too late to turn from the darkness of that cave and walk out into the light, but the more time spent in darkness, the more difficult and painful it can be to leave.

We can sometimes feel trapped in the depressing darkness of our situations. It sometimes seems as if the past has already determined our future. Even the bible says "*...I, the Lord your God, am a jealous God, punishing the children for the sins of the parents to the third and fourth generation...*" (Exodus 20:5). This was initially a difficult truth for me to accept, until I realized that it is not a threat, but a warning. The past might influence and shape my future, but I have the ability to choose. Regardless of the behaviours modeled for me and the incorrect assumptions I chose to believe, even though they were reinforced from an early age, I can be different. There are numerous accounts of sons in the lineage of Israel's kings who did a complete one-eighty from what their fathers had modeled, and God responded to them according to their own hearts. I no longer believe my earlier incorrect assumption that God holds me to account for the sins of my father, just as He does not hold you to account for the sins of your mother, father, or anyone else. There are simply natural consequences to the choices I've made and the false beliefs I've held as a result of my reaction to the situation. I want you to know that God wants you to know there is unconditional acceptance to which we can all find our way. In order to get there, we must sometimes realize that it is preposterous to *not* question the beliefs that took hold in our minds at an early age.

During those two years before my family moved away, I internalized the message that something was wrong with me. My father had left us, and being the latest addition to our family, I was likely the cause or he would have done it sooner. My older brothers must have known this as well, which had to be why they preferred spending time with one another than with me. My mother had to work two jobs to support three children on her own, but it never occurred to me that her work schedule must have been exhausting. No, her reluctance to spend time together must have been because I wasn't worth spending time with. Even my best friend would abandon me in favour of the cool kids when the opportunity arose. My apparent worthlessness became a core belief, a foundation on which I began to build walls.

In spite of our physical relocation, it was as if the true identity which had been originally intended for me was somehow left behind. There was simply no room for it amongst the baggage I had already begun to accumulate.

More Than Words Can Say

"That leaves only me to blame 'cause Mama tried" – Merle Haggard

"FINE THEN, I'll just throw it in the garbage!" With these words, my mother threw the Scrabble set down the nearby basement stairs. The duct tape which was struggling to hold together the ancient, disintegrating box, as well as that which was barely holding two flaps together as one game board finally tore free. The sound of the wooden tiles first rattling against one another during their downward journey, followed by their chorus of clickety-clacks across the concrete floor then crescendoed into a brief moment of complete silence. Lacking any words to suit the situation, and also no longer possessing the letters to make them up, I turned and walked out the door, slamming it behind myself as if the rattling door frame conveyed all the shock and awe of a seven letter word atop a triple word score.

That scene was not exactly the culmination of years of my desire for independence battling against my mother's apparent desire to shelter me from the world. It was, however, a definite watershed moment. It was like that scene in many movies when after persevering through numerous tribulations, the protagonist has reached a place of peace and tranquility. Things are going well, and it seems that things will continue to go well, but then something happens. Our hero says or does something stupid. An antagonist interferes. A supporting character reveals something about the protagonist to the co-lead which alters their perception and changes their course away from happily ever after. We've seen it time and again on both the big and small screen. In one episode of Friends, Ross and Rachel had patched things up, only for her to soon find out that Ross had slept with another woman, and *"We were on a break!"* doesn't cut it as a suitable excuse. In The Wizard of Oz, Dorothy and her friends finally reached the Emerald City and were granted audience with Oz the Great and Powerful, only to be turned away on a dangerous quest to earn their respective requests. And in Unfatherless, Sean failed to recognize the true meaning behind his mother's seemingly nonchalant suggestion that he pack her Scrabble board along with the rest of the things he was steadily accumulating for his first apartment.

Spoiler alerts: Ross and Rachel did eventually end up together. Dorothy and her friends vanquished the remaining wicked witch, thus fulfilling their end of the deal and forcing the Wizard to reciprocate. And as for me, well, I'm still alive. There are an unknown number of remaining scenes to play out. I cannot press the pause button mid-stream to see the remaining minutes in which this story must reach a conclusion. I certainly cannot rewind and change anything that has occurred. But have you ever read a story or watched a movie for the second, third, or nineteenth time and noticed something that you had not noticed before? We can do that. We can rewrite our reactions and perceptions based upon the understanding we now have. Revisiting and recounting events allows us a point of view different than that of one of the participants. In the moment, I reacted to my mother's obvious anger by following the script which had developed over the years: get out, wait for her to cool down, and apologize later. In retrospect, succumbing to the same old subconscious routines may not have been the best choice, because it may not have been anger that we were dealing with. We all too often react to what we think we see rather than what is actually there.

I can only imagine the reaction of those at the foot of the cross, watching Jesus' slow, agonizing death when he cried out, *"My God, my God, why have you forsaken me?"* (Matthew 27:46). Had I been exposed to the bible at a younger age, I most likely would have projected my own feelings of abandonment onto Jesus in this scenario, and my own belief of a father onto God. It would have been natural to draw those parallels and perpetuate my paradigm that fathers abandon their sons. It would have been quite easy for me to assume that if God could abandon Jesus, then He could abandon me without so much as a second thought. Not only would I have viewed this scene as God abandoning Jesus, but also as Jesus abandoning his disciples. After all, He had allowed Himself to be arrested and taken to His inevitable execution. It may have taken me a second, third, or nineteenth look to see the truth. How many times did Jesus' followers who were present for His horrific death have to replay the scene in their minds before realizing the truth?

The truth is, God has never forsaken Jesus, nor me, nor you, regardless of what we might see, believe, or feel. One of Jesus' many names is "Rabbi", which means "teacher". Jesus continued to teach right up to His final breath. Uttering those words, "*My God, my God, why have you forsaken me?*" would have sparked the memory of anyone present who had knowledge of scripture, because it was actually a quote of Psalm 22:1. That Psalm goes on to say that Israel trusted God, and He delivered them from calamity. That they cried out and were saved. Psalm 22 says "*my bones are out of joint*" (14), "*my mouth is dried up*" (15), "*a pack of villains encircles me; they pierce my hands and feet*" (16), "*they cast lots for my garment*" (18), all things which happened to Jesus while He was on the cross. And Psalm 22 goes on to say that God IS listening, that He has NOT turned away, that "*the poor will eat and be satisfied*" (26). The author of this Psalm, Jesus' ancestor King David, concludes this particular song with "*They will proclaim His righteousness, declaring to a people yet unborn: He has done it!*" (Psalm 22:31). "*He has done it*", or in other words, as uttered by Jesus from the cross soon after that other statement, "*It is finished*" (John 19:30). In spite of the truth, had I been at the foot of the literal cross, I'm sure I would have felt abandoned by Jesus for allowing Himself to be taken away to certain death. It is often only in hindsight that we see the truth.

It's ironic that one of the earliest memories I have of my mother is one of her abandoning me, because in retrospect, I know she never has. This particular situation began after a long day toiling away at the drudgery of basic grade one arithmetic and spelling, when the glorious sound of the school bell finally rang out. Amid the clamour of chair legs scraping the floor, books slamming shut, and my classmates and I beginning our own conversations, any instructions our teacher may have been trying to relay to the class were lost. Of course, who should need any instruction other than that of the bell ringing? It was time to GO.

It seemed as if somehow, neither my brothers nor Ryan had received the memo. I was waiting in our usual spot outside the front door of our school with none of them in sight. If that hadn't been enough of a red flag for me, the lack of other students exiting the building ought to have tipped me off to the fact that something was unusual about my current situation. Just as a lot of us do many times in life though, even if some part of me noticed that I was the exception to the norm, I assumed that everyone else must be wrong, not me. I'm glad now that I'm older and more mature, I no longer make that assumption; I know for a fact that I'm never wrong. After what must have been hours of waiting for them, my impatience grew to a degree which led me to the decision that I was competent enough to walk the three and a half blocks back home all by myself, and so that is exactly what I did. I do not recall exactly how I felt, but I can just imagine the pride I had in myself when I crossed that stained front walk of our home. I bounded up the front steps, pulled open the screen door, and twisted the knob of the inner door; except, I didn't. The knob would not turn. I was locked out. In spite of yet another unusual occurrence adding to this chain of events, I remained unphased. Undeterred, I ran around to the back of the house, only to find yet another locked door. My mother must have simply forgotten to leave it open, so I first began to knock, and then pound on the door, but to no avail. What could I do, other than sit there on the doorstep with my face in my hands, and begin to cry? It had become obvious that my mother had picked up my brothers from school and run off with them, abandoning me. After all, *"I'm not good enough for anyone to care about"*.

However, after some unknown length of time spent in that misery, there was such care in the tone of her voice when I suddenly heard my mother ask, "what are you doing at home?" as she stepped out of the garage, placed the grocery bags she had been carrying on the ground, and reached out for me. After whatever length of time it took for me to calm down in her embrace, I found the words to explain that I had walked home from school at the end of the day all by myself. "End of the day?" she responded, "it's barely afternoon, that must have been the lunch bell". Well, no wonder then, that on top of everything else I'd been feeling, I was also hungry.

After that day, I never again accidentally left school early. Of course, I must emphasize that word, 'accidentally', because I never did develop a healthy relationship with school. My mother certainly did her part, playing the role of alarm clock with enough time to ensure I started the day with breakfast. I always had clean clothes to wear and a lunch to stow in the backpack which also carried the homework I had been forced to complete on time. The disciplines that she put in place for my brothers and me became automatic, default behaviours. They became routines to be followed without question, which I did for a time. Even once life came to the point when her work schedule demanded that our mother leave the house earlier than I needed to be awake, an actual alarm clock with a loud buzzer had replaced her morning yell, I mean – her gentle morning nudge, and I had been conditioned to obey the shrill, piercing sound. I had also developed the skill of pouring cereal into a bowl and covering it with milk; a skill which I am proud to say I have retained to this very day. Of course, being the youngest of three children helped to ensure that I did as I was told, considering those two additional voices in my life who seemed to believe they had some kind of authority over me. I had learned a strange kind of pseudo-independence, having reached an age where I could do a lot more things for myself, yet all of those things were imposed upon me rather than a product of my own self determination. Some part of me began to realize that even though rules were to be followed, I had a choice. I could rebel against any supposed authority, perhaps including a *"you can't tell me what to do, you're not my father!"* as a part of my disobedience, and deal with the consequences later. Consequences are Future Sean's problem. On the other hand, I could be kind to my future self, do as I was told, and potentially reap a reward.

There was one year when my mother and her then-boyfriend had decided their relationship was serious enough that we should all live together. I honestly do not recall having any feelings toward this man, neither positive nor negative, only ambivalence. He seemed much more interested in a relationship with our mother than with my brothers and me. At seven or eight years old, I definitely had negative feelings about moving away from the only home I had ever known, regardless of what had happened there. We were relocating to a house on the outskirts of a nearby small town, perhaps a half hour drive outside of the city. There are drives which take five to ten minutes as an adult which I recall seeming like hours as a child, so at the time a half hour drive might as well have been a cross country trek. The one friend I had would be completely out of reach, and of course in my absence he would forget about my existence altogether. Somehow, the fact that I was the one leaving still made me feel as though I was being abandoned.

This new home was just far enough outside of the nearby town that even though a short bike ride would bring my brothers and me within its limits, the ride did entail travelling along a two-lane highway to get there. In spite of having completed the mandatory bicycle safety course at school, and regardless of being able to demonstrate my ability to keep to a straight line and use all of the correct hand signals at all of the proper times, my mother imposed the rule that I could not endeavor upon this journey alone. This left me in a position of my brothers' mercy, which was a truly special gift thanks to its incredible rarity. On the occasions when they, either as a unit or singularly, would ride to town, they generally had their own agenda of which I was not a part. As I had already learned, being the youngest of three boys came with certain disadvantages. Even if I had not already developed a predisposition to perceive the slightest lack of inclusion as abandonment, it would have hurt to have been consistently left out.

It was during this time, however, when I began to realize that being the youngest of three boys, otherwise known as the "baby", also came with certain advantages. I also began to learn, whether accurately or not, that advantages can often come with strings attached. At minimum, it's reasonable for a person to expect or even request basic respect in return for their positive treatment of you. At their worst, these strings are like those held by a puppeteer, manipulating every possible movement of their marionette. Even the most giving, loving person can have blind-spots about their self which lead to some subconscious expectation of reciprocity to their benevolence. Sometimes, as was the case for me, those of us being treated advantageously will attach strings to ourselves which were never intended by the other party to be there. Being left out by my brothers while still too young to be left on my own meant that mom was often the only one left to entertain me, to find ways to occupy my time, and to ensure my survival through basic disciplines such as not wandering out into traffic again.

Over the course of time, spending many occasions alone with my mother, I began to learn that certain behaviours would lead to certain rewards. It didn't occur to my childish mind that instilling those behaviours within me was a normal part of raising a child. Nor did it seem to cross my mind that what I viewed as rewards were often normal acts of love and kindness. I attached strings and made correlations where there ought not to have been any. Saying "please" and "thank you", and being otherwise well-mannered is basic respect which should be attached to human interaction a lot more often than it seems to be. Furthermore, rewarding excellence, and I daresay punishing wrongdoing for that matter, can be a fantastic way to encourage desired behaviours and to discourage undesired behaviours. Sometimes making a connection between a behaviour and a result is good if done intentionally, and if the behaviour, result, and connection are made clear. Our subconscious minds can sometimes twist this concept and make us believe that we must act or be a certain way in order to be accepted or loved. We can feel insecure about the idea that someone may love us for who we are, and so we try to earn that love through what we do.

Although I felt lonely a lot of the time, I wasn't completely alone in my state of pseudo-independence during this season of life. The previous owner of our new home had moved to an apartment which did not allow pets, and so we had inherited a medium sized, middle aged mutt named Finnigan. One day, when my mother needed to take a trip into town to run a few errands, I had to be brought along because apparently Finnigan was not a suitable babysitter. I insisted that he be allowed to come along, and one of the advantages of being "the baby" is that you often get your way. The caveat to bringing the dog along was that as mom would visit each store, I would then have to wait in the car with him so that we could leave the windows open. I cannot speak directly for God, but if there's anyone He does not actually love, it might be people who leave dogs alone in hot cars with the windows up. I must have done a good job watching the dog, because when mom came out from the final stop on our journey, that small-town combination store where you can get nearly anything, she handed me a couple Archie books. Not the comic-sized, thin, done in a minute comic books either. These were the Archie digests with somewhere between one to two hundred pages each!

When we returned home, after obediently helping to carry in the various shopping bags which had resulted from this trip, Finnigan and I disappeared to my bedroom where I could quietly read with him curled up next to me. I was eager to do so, but also knew that mom would want some peace and quiet to put away the groceries and deal with whatever other purchases she had made. My mother can be a task-oriented person, and to this day I suspect those Archie digests were a bribe to keep me out from underfoot while she focussed on her priorities. Being a child who was reading at the level of chat bubbles rather than reading between the lines, it didn't consciously occur to me even as this became a pattern that I wasn't the priority. That lie was simply implanted into my subconscious the way an enemy plants a mine in a field, hidden until some future misstep leads to an explosion.

Over the weeks and months which followed, as I steadily accumulated an entire shelf full of Archie digests, I learned that quiet, unquestioning obedience would often result in tangible reward. My paradigm of good behaviour was shaped by my mother's apparent needs and desires; nothing that she ever expressed, simply those which I assumed were true, whether they actually were or not. If I had to be taken along to the grocery store, I should make things easier by handling the cart, and loading and unloading bags. When I was left behind by my brothers yet again, I should entertain myself so that she could watch her shows or do whatever it was adults do. I created associations in my mind between the supposed rewards, mostly books, and the idea that I had to repay my mother for those rewards by perpetuating those good behaviours, or by simply allowing her to focus on other priorities. I attached strings where she never intended them.

I now know that from my mother's perspective, her introverted youngest child loved to read. Though we didn't have a lot of money, books were one thing she could afford to give as a gift on a somewhat regular basis, whether because they were inexpensive Archie digests, or the second hand paperbacks to which I quickly graduated. She was right. I was developing a love for reading, and even somewhat of a liking for solitude. Even though I sometimes deserved the opposite due to a lack of obedience or because of my outright misbehaviour, the gifts didn't stop. Yes, there were negative consequences when I did something wrong. The negative consequences were always temporary, and nothing I did ever cancelled out my mother's desire to give me good things. She was not attaching strings to these gifts. She had no expectation of "quid pro quo". She was graciously giving a free gift, out of love. I had done nothing to earn the gifts, nor the love.

In Matthew 19:16 – 22, there is a story of a man who asks Jesus what he has to do to have eternal life. To paraphrase, Jesus tells him, "*Keep the commandments. Don't kill people, don't commit adultery, don't steal or lie. Honour your parents, and love your neighbour*". The man says that he's done all of those things, and asks what else is necessary, to which Jesus says, paraphrasing again, "*sell everything you own, donate the proceeds to charity, and follow me if you want to be perfect*". In the first part of Jesus' answer, He's prescribing basic things. At least, not killing someone ought to be a basic way of life, yet here we are. Regardless of our failures, Jesus is saying that eternal life with Him is attainable.

He lists out a few of the Ten Commandments from the Old Testament, but those commandments basically all boil down to two things: love God and love other people. The man in this story doesn't seem to understand. He thinks there must be strings attached. It's almost as if he *wants* there to be a more difficult path to eternal life so that he can brag about earning it when he gets there. Jesus gives this man exactly what he seems to want. It isn't a one-size-fits-all answer. We're not all called to give everything away. Jesus tailored His answer to speak directly to this man's heart, but the general question is whether we are willing to prioritize Him over stuff. The man walks off feeling dejected, because although he thought there must be some way to earn his way into Heaven, he didn't want to have to go that far. Giving up his fortune, that which was most dear to his heart, in return for a relationship seemed too unreasonable for this man. If he couldn't do something which he feels is reasonable in order to receive his reward, he might as well give up altogether.

Would I have given up my books in exchange to just spend time with my father? Perhaps, but I'm not certain I would have. In that particular season of life my feelings about him had been blanketed by a cold, still rage, much as a fresh snow blankets a field. My yearning was becoming less like a compass needle pointing toward the set destination of this man who had abandoned me, and more like a weathervane, trying to find direction in the midst of swirling winds.

Would I have given up my books in exchange to just spend time with my mother? I don't know, and I didn't ever have to face that choice. Regardless of my assumption that I was not a priority to her, she was available to me on a regular basis. The countless hours spent with my books were also a means of education as I began to read above my level and learn new words. One of my favourite books was the dictionary. One time, as I was pulling it off the bookshelf in our living room my mother asked, "*how many words do you know now?*" I should have known better than to respond that I probably already knew more than her. "*Oh, really?*" she responded. "*Well then, let's see how you do at this. Wait here.*" She disappeared somewhere in the house, and returned with a Scrabble set in hand. We sat at the dining room table and she began to explain how this game was played. I was enthralled. It took at least a couple of years before I finally beat her for the first time, but even though she was a sore loser, we continued to play on a regular basis. My brothers were never interested in this game, and neither were any friends of hers. This was our thing. This was a special time between the two of us. The gift of words had planted seeds which grew into a relationship.

Neither of us knew that one day, my mother would want me to take a tangible representation of these memories along when I moved out, but that time was coming. She would offer this very same Scrabble set, as if to say, *"share this with someone, and when you do, remember my love"*. In ignorance, I would tell her that I had moved on, and that she could keep her memories to herself. Not in so many words, but in essence. If you've played Scrabble, you might know that it is often better to resist your first thought. If you exercise some patience, pay close attention to the words that have already been played, and put thoughtful, careful consideration into your next words, you are more likely to come out ahead. Obviously, I had not yet learned to apply that lesson to life.

Sometimes, we simply do not have the words to express what it is we're feeling. I think this is one of the reasons *"the Holy Spirit helps us in our weakness. We do not know what we ought to pray for, but Spirit Himself intercedes for us through wordless groans"* (Romans 8:26). I did not know what to pray for other than a father, and I had already given up on ever receiving that gift. Had I known at the time that *"everyone who asks, receives; the one who seeks finds; and to the one who knocks, the door will be opened."* (Luke 11:10), I might have been more persistent and courageous enough to venture the short distance home, to my Heavenly Father's house, across that blood-stained threshold. There would have been no sitting on the doorstep, face in hands, crying. I can just imagine the pride He would have had in His eyes when He opened the door to my knocking, because I know it now. Except at the time, I didn't. It was still years before I found the direction in which my hunger would finally be sated.

Hand-Me-Downs

"Maybe you just know what you've been told over and over and over again." –
Robert Ludlum, *The Bourne Identity*

Allegedly, I'm an adult now. I'm not completely sure when or how that happened, but somewhere along the line, it did. At least, physically; I do still laugh at some rather immature jokes. Some people might say that adulthood began when I turned eighteen years old, some might say it was when I moved out of my mother's house. One young adult I know once said that she knew she was an adult when, for the first time in her own apartment, she realized that she could have ice cream for dinner. There was nobody to stop her, it was all her decision, and she knew the consequence of feeling obligated to spend additional time on her treadmill the next day. Some would say that eating ice cream for dinner is not an adult-like thing to do at all, but that's not the point. It's the realization of being responsible for one's own decisions and owning that responsibility which is the sign of maturity in this example. I think that it's okay to occasionally crash on the couch with a tub of Rocky Road after work because cooking is just too hard that day. Immaturity would be doing it on a too-regular basis, and / or ignoring that there are consequences to your actions. The childish thing to do is to blame your poor decision on your mood, or on the person or circumstance which led you to that mood. Whether you call it maturing from childhood to adulthood, becoming a new creation in Christ, or attaining a new level of self-actualization, maturity is tied to our emotional, mental, and spiritual sides just as much as it is to our physical bodies, perhaps more. Our ability to reason and decide, to exercise free will, is what sets humanity apart from other species. I believe there is even an additional level of maturity where we question whether our choices are made out of our own free will, or if they are simply the decisions we've been trained to make.

A friend of mine once decided to quit a job where he was being treated unfairly. He had been working in the same place for just under twenty years, and when certain circumstances outside of his control changed, he realized it was time to part ways with this particular company. He worked out his notice period (like a mature adult), and then said his goodbyes on a Friday afternoon. The following Monday morning, he woke up at his usual time, followed his usual shower, shave, and dress routine, and drove to work. It was only once he pulled into the parking lot of the company where he no longer worked that he realized he was not supposed to be there. He returned home, quickly forgiving himself for such a mistake, because he knew that a habit formed over nearly two decades has a certain power. It was after doing the exact same thing again the next morning when he came to the conclusion that a conscious effort to break his normal routine would be necessary. If he did repeat his mistake that Wednesday morning, he won't admit it to me. This may be a more extreme example of an auto-pilot behaviour, to the point where you cannot imagine doing the same thing. We all do things though, which out of repetition take no conscious thought to do, and even take conscious thought to not do.

When I was learning to drive, I had to pay conscious attention to every little detail. How much pressure I was using on the gas pedal, the exact distance to move my foot to the brake, where to find the lever to signal a turn or a lane change, and many other things. I know this is a surprise to many people, but yes, cars are equipped with a blinking light on either side, both front and back, which you can use to indicate to other drivers when you intend to turn or change lanes. After years of experience, thinking about how most of these actions have become automatic for me, and likely for others as well, is actually somewhat frightening. We share the road with dozens, or even hundreds of other people each day, most of whom are navigating a mass of nearly two metric tons at speeds possibly reaching over 100 kilometers per hour, on auto-pilot. It's amazing there aren't more collisions than already occur. Similarly, we encounter people on a daily basis who may be displaying attitudes or acting out behaviours which are just as automatic, and sometimes just as dangerous.

There is a strange phenomenon that seems to affect anybody who begins to drive a new car. I don't recall ever noticing a Ford Escape on the road until my wife and I bought one, but now they're everywhere. I know everybody wants to be like me, but it's astounding how many I actually see. The truth is they were there all along, I just never noticed before owning my own. In my experience, negative behaviours work in the opposite way. Rather than knowing of our own shortcomings and then seeing them everywhere around us, we don't easily recognize our own issues without some outside catalyst. If we tend to see the same irritating or bothersome behaviour or attitude in many of the people we encounter throughout our daily routines, there is a good chance that they are actually reflecting an issue of our own back to us. The temptation is sometimes to help others relieve themselves of that particular piece of baggage, but we have no right to do so while navigating through life with two metric tons of our own baggage. Coming to the realization that we have been carrying certain negative behaviours and taking responsibility for them is a sign of maturity. It can often be easier to let go of an immature behaviour, attitude, or belief if we know where we first picked it up.

As the youngest of three growing boys, I certainly didn't have a shortage of new clothes. That is, clothes which were new to me. As various garments were outgrown by my brothers, they became mine. Once in a while, it was a treat to be bequeathed a particular coveted item, but for the most part I viewed this as an injustice. To rarely get anything that is actually new, to have no choice in style, or colour, or pattern, and to be forced into acceptance of the wear and tear that has already occurred was dreadfully unfair in my view. Thankfully, shoes, socks, and most importantly, underwear were exceptions to this rule. For the most part though, I viewed my mother's thriftiness not as the logical budgeting decision it was, but as yet another way in which I was unworthy. To this day, in spite of being able to afford to refresh my wardrobe on a regular basis, I hesitate to do so. I have no problem ensuring that I have presentable clothes when older items have come to the point of becoming a car-washing rag, but it typically does take that long. I have no problem indulging in everyday purchases, such as fostering my Starbucks addiction, but larger, or even medium purchases tend to require a significant reason. Part of the reason for this is because as an adult, I now see the logic behind setting and adhering to a budget. If the clothes I have are even the least bit suitable, there is no reason to replace them. After all, I earned the holes in my jeans, and I certainly don't mean through the effort of using a pair of scissors on them. It just isn't logical to throw away and replace something from which I can still find use. Though, as much as I pride myself on my Vulcan-like adherence to logic, I must also admit that the human part of me still questions whether I am worth extraneous expenditures.

Clothing is not all that was handed down to me from my brothers. In the absence of a father, they were the most present and prevalent male role models after whom I patterned behaviour in my younger years. I somehow overlooked the obvious fact that they also didn't have a father, and therefore may not have always been the best examples to follow. Though you may not have siblings, or they may not be older than you, there are multiple sources in all of our lives from where we've learned how to be who we are. Family members, schoolmates, co-workers, or even country songs and soap operas can influence us to either accept or discard behaviours and attitudes that we deem appropriate to either emulate or disregard. Regardless of the source, chances are neither you nor I made a conscious decision to adopt each and every behaviour or attitude which was handed down to us. In our desire to be accepted, we often subconsciously mimic those from whom we desire acceptance in order to fit in. There is an inherent fear that if we rock the boat, we'll be left with an abandoned ship.

Another form of thriftiness my mother exercised was to not pay for a babysitter from as early a time as possible. Big Brother is two years older than Middle Brother, and five years older than me, which meant by the time I was seven years old our mother had free childcare. In that era of toy guns in use at a public park not causing neighbours to call the police, there was also little to no concern about certification in babysitting. Looking back, I can understand why such certification is now deemed necessary. Just as I know that grass is green and the sky is blue, you should know that boys do immature things and get in trouble. I don't recall exactly whose idea it was to play on the train bridge that was just a couple of blocks away from our house that one time, but I do know it could not possibly have been mine. I certainly wasn't the one who decided that Big Brother and Middle Brother should take handfuls of the medium-sized stones from beside the tracks and drop them over the edge. I will admit that it was my decision to mimic them and participate in this newfound game. Did I mention that this particular train bridge was above the underpass of a rather busy road? It seemed as though the sound of stones bouncing off the roofs of the cars below would amuse us to no end, until one car with a cracked windshield found its way to the correct side-street that would bring it to our location. Although there was no rock-solid evidence that any of us had caused the damage to the very angry man's windshield, our mere presence in that location was obviously enough for him. We knew our guilt, and so in spite of my brothers' complete silence in the face of his yelling, as the weak link I blurted out a confession. At that point one of my brothers grabbed my arm, yanked me forward, and we ran faster than I could ever have imagined possible. We never did see that angry man again, but we did notice a police car patrolling the neighbourhood later that day. Mom, if this is the first time you're hearing this story, I'm sorry. It won't happen again.

In the following days and even weeks, I spent a lot of time in solitary confinement. My apparent punishment for so easily ratting out my brothers was to be abandoned by them to any degree which was possible. Though neither of them intended to teach me that you never admit to anything unless you're caught red-handed, I certainly didn't learn the value of integrity. What I did learn was a distorted, shadow version of loyalty. In a healthy form, loyalty is a good thing. It helps to build mutual respect and admiration. It helps to build trust. It is one of the defining characteristics of a stable relationship. Mutual loyalty between people who do not abuse or manipulate one another is an integral component to making each other feel accepted and loved. Thank God that He later redeemed my blind, immature loyalty, helping me to build it anew on a firm foundation of values. The shadow version that I had initially developed was a codependent behaviour; an acceptance and even a perpetuation of other people's negative behaviours in order to gain their acceptance. Learning that I could be so easily excluded from my brothers' activities if I were to betray their trust, I ensured my inclusion by resolving to always be on their side. This meant that I was not only alongside for certain delinquent escapades, but I was enabling their BS (boyish shenanigans) by not bringing them to light. I had many opportunities to choose to be honest when I was asked how something had broken or gone missing, where a mess had come from, or why we were late coming home from school and where we had been. In those moments, I had come to believe it was better to claim, *"I don't know"*, *"not me"*, or to offer up the lies we had rehearsed. In spite of intrinsically knowing that telling the truth was the right thing to do, and also in spite of the gentle whisper of conscience convicting me for being complicit, I believed that remaining loyal to my brothers would guarantee that we would always be there for one another. I was wrong.

After some time of enjoying the conditional acceptance I was awarded for mimicking my brothers, it may come as no surprise to you that I wanted something better. It may sound familiar when compared to your own story. Those of us who have a hard time finding acceptance often come to a point where simply participating is not enough for us to feel a sense of security in our relationships. Whether true or not, I had already learned and come to believe that an individual in the role of follower lessens in worth as the leader gains popularity. There is a reason that large organizations have large hierarchies. The CEO cannot possibly devote time and energy to directly manage, lead, and develop every front-line worker as the organization grows. They generally have a team of vice presidents reporting to them, an inner circle they directly disciple. With the education and employment experience that qualifies one for nothing other than a front-line position, an individual is not likely to be a part of that inner circle. Who would recruit and entrust a mere fisherman to start and lead a worldwide organization? In the same way, when we are in a relationship where what we have to give is not good enough, we sometimes look for ways in which we can upgrade or even embellish our credentials. There also seems to be a direct correlation between the depths of our desire for acceptance, and the lengths to which we will go to make ourselves appear qualified or worthy.

Have I mentioned my mother's thriftiness? The concept of an allowance was something I had only heard of from other children; the ones who were worth the ability and freedom to purchase themselves treats from the corner store or the ice cream truck. After numerous opportunities to be the one person in the group not able to participate, or to be left out from the group altogether as others caught on that the only way I was getting a chocolate bar or bag of chips was on their dime, I was determined to find a way to change the situation. For the record, these things did cost more than a dime when I was a child. I'm not *that* old, it's just a saying. Too young to be legally employed and short on means to earn money when there was always somebody better at mowing lawns or shoveling snow, the most apparent option was to take money from my mother's purse. At first it was just the minimal amount required so that I could be a part of the group. As long as the frequency and quantity both remained low, it seemed to me that I could perpetuate this indiscretion indefinitely without notice or consequence. One of the problems with actually getting away with this kind of thing is it tempts us to test how much *more* we can get away with; much like an addict moving on to harder drugs or greater quantities, we escalate. Over time, the frequency of my thefts and the quantity increased. Part of my justification for this was to increase my personal value; if I could buy things not only for myself, but also for others, then theoretically I would be elevated in the social hierarchy. I would have more to give, which I believed would increase my worth to others. Ironically, in my quest for that result, I was decreasing my self-worth because I knew all along that the end did not justify the means.

There was no reason for anyone outside of our family to know the truth of where I was getting the money, but my brothers knew they weren't receiving an allowance. Before they could make the assumption that I was being treated favourably and question our mother about it, thus exposing my thefts, and knowing that I could trust them in the same way that I had shown they can trust me, I told them the truth. They were surprisingly accepting of this, but of course it was a conditional acceptance. Not only would I now be required to include them in reaping the rewards of my crime, there also came demands that I perpetuate this behaviour more often than I had already. Keeping up a higher frequency and quantity, none of us ought to have been surprised when the day of reckoning finally came.

When I first started reading the bible much later in life, one of the things about Jesus that caused me to like Him was His obvious distaste for hypocrisy. He warns people not to follow the example of certain overzealous religious leaders, because *"they tie up heavy, cumbersome loads and put them on other people's shoulders, but they themselves are not willing to lift a finger to move them"* (Matthew 23:4). I have met a lot of people who say that hypocrisy is unacceptable, but I don't seem to have met nearly as many people whose actions display the same sentiment. It didn't occur to me at the time that my brothers were insisting that I take a load on my own shoulders while they were not willing to lift a finger, I was just glad to be in their good graces. Even now, I'm certain there was no intent to make me the scapegoat, and that they were simply taking advantage of an opportunity which had presented itself. It does, however, strike me that from a young age, hypocrisy can come so easily and even unintentionally to us humans.

I can still remember how my heart sank, after nearly an hour of intense interrogation. Our mother had returned home livid after experiencing the embarrassment of trying to pay a car repair bill, only to find that she was twenty dollars short after withdrawing the exact amount of cash needed only one day prior. When the yelling was eventually done and we were left alone to anticipate the severity of our impending punishment, I quickly pointed out to my brothers that as long as none of us admitted to anything, we could not all be blamed. I don't recall which of them it was who then called for our mother and informed her that I had the twenty dollar bill in my pocket at that exact moment, but the betrayal broke me. My brother's betrayal of me, though tremendously hurtful, was actually the least of my heartbreak. The truly soul shattering self-condemnation came from the look on our mother's face as she pulled the bill from my pocket and realized my betrayal of her. In that moment, I came to believe that I could not trust anyone, including myself.

In hindsight, I cannot and do not blame my brothers for any of the hand-me-down attitudes or behaviours which I came to own. They were just as fatherless, abandoned, and lost as I was. I also cannot and do not blame the immature ignorance of my young self for setting course away from my intended path, as easy as it might be. Placing blame is unproductive and immature. The productive, mature, adult thing to do is to realize that if we want things to change, we need to do something different. I cannot justify a life lived chained in darkness, feeling unforgivable. Even if I could somehow justify living such a mediocre existence, the simple acknowledgment that it needs justification should tell me that it is not right. In spite of the numerous scenarios through which unhealthy behaviours were modeled for me, the mature thing to do is to realize the responsibility I had in adopting those behaviours. The adult thing to do is to accept what I can now see in a clear, normal mirror; to leave my child-like chains of assumption behind and walk toward the light. I have forgiven myself for the trouble I got into as a child, and the trouble I caused. To not do so would be to claim that I know better than God, who knew what I would do and chose to love me regardless.

If I could travel back through time and tell my young self that he is loved and forgiven, I doubt he would listen to me. It would take divine intervention to break those chains.

How Do I Get There?

"We can easily forgive a child who is afraid of the dark; the real tragedy of life is when men are afraid of the light" – Plato

I hate moving. To be clear, I'm not talking about all moving, even though my runner's knees might beg to differ. I have learned to gain some sick satisfaction from putting myself through the regular punishment of push-ups, sit-ups, and various other torture methods disguised as exercise. I actually pay real money to contribute to a gymnasium rental to play volleyball, the one sport for which my long, thin frame was always somewhat well suited. There's also something about the wind in my face as I pedal my bicycle at speeds bordering upon dangerous which calms me like nothing else. Some moving is good, and is good for you, and has good results. To be precise, I should say that I hate relocating; that is, moving to a new home. You may have similar feelings if you have been through at least one move that included any number of detestable tasks. Begging local stores for any empty cardboard boxes they have. Arranging not only for the three or five tonne truck, but also finding a person with the confidence to drive it. Bribing your friends with the promise of pizza and beer at the end of the day if only they would show up to help, and of course the frantic last minute calls for extra help when at least one of the original crew flakes out. Navigating large pieces of furniture through doorways and sometimes up or down stairways, repeatedly yelling "PIVOT!" in order to fit the pieces around tricky corners. One time, I even had the corner of a freezer dropped on my hand, tearing the entire nail off of my pinky finger. The only thing worse than moving is helping someone else move. The whole ordeal is best left to professionals.

The last time my wife and I moved, we made it as easy on ourselves as possible. We hired movers to come with their truck, and to do all of the loading and unloading. We rented plastic bins which, all being identical, would stack perfectly both when open and empty awaiting their cargo, and when full. We even used colour coordinated zip ties to close the bins in order to easily identify the room of the new house into which they should be placed. I know, we're a couple of nerds. Every little detail was planned, and though everything went according to plan, somehow there were still anxieties throughout the experience. Packing up shouldn't be difficult, until the inevitable question arises: *"should we keep this?"* Navigating the discussion that ensues should also be easy, but could send even the most cohesive couples to counselling. When the movers show up, standing aside and allowing them to do their thing shouldn't be difficult, but I don't like feeling useless. Of course I'm going to help load the truck, because what kind of real man sits around drinking coffee while three young guys are doing all of the work for him? And then, while unpacking over the next few days... OK, who am I kidding? While unpacking over the next few weeks, and even months, the worst part of all is the question: *"why did we keep this?"*

I don't recall having to deal with any of these issues as a child, in spite of moving multiple times. Prior to my teenage years when I became capable of helping to carry things, I remember having only two concerns. The first was which bedroom would be mine, but being the youngest and weakest that choice was made for me anyway. The other was something with which I'm sure you're familiar: I was going to be the new kid on the block, and not one of those cool new kids who could sing, dance, and sell millions of albums. I just didn't have the right stuff, baby. One particular move, however, had a silver lining. During the year we had spent outside of the city, Ryan had also relocated, and when we moved back into the city it was to the same area where he now resided! We would be in the same school once again, and within a short bike ride of one another.

The excitement of reuniting with my old best friend overrode any apprehension I may have had about having to start over yet again, and trying to fit in and prove the worth that I didn't even believe I had. Having already gone through the new kid experience before, showing up as an outsider and bringing all of my shortcomings along, I knew it could be an uphill battle. As adults it seems that the new people we meet are interested in our occupation; one of the first questions we ask and are often asked is *"what do you do?"* It's as if a person's job is the main contributing factor to their identity. As children who have not yet embarked upon careers of our own, the line of questioning when getting to know one another often turns to family. Especially among young boys, it seems to me that our identity was closely associated with that of our father, and whether my dad can beat up your dad. If he was strong, you must be strong. If he was athletic, you must be athletic. If he was rich, or brave, or handsome, or some combination of these things, you were much more likely to be popular. If your father was a policeman or a firefighter, you were superhuman. If your father was a murderer, you were superhuman as long as the other boys believed your lie that he was a policeman or a firefighter.

That first summer back in the city, having aged slightly and now living where there was no highway in between our home and any destination I may have had, I was afforded a new level of independence. Ryan and I no longer lived on the same block like we previously had, but we were about a five minute bike ride apart. Throughout the too few weeks before another school year began, we picked up pretty much where we had left off. Although he had a head start in this new area of the city and had already made some new friends, we spent a great deal of time together. If not for all of my insecurities, I might have been able to believe he had also missed my company. However, it wasn't long before I unpacked my codependence, my sense of unworthiness, and my fear of abandonment. I was not yet emotionally or mentally mature enough to recognize this baggage and ask, *"why did I keep this?"*

To me, having even one friend was a special thing. The fact that there was no longer the circumstantial imposition of friendship that had existed before, that lack of options back when we had lived on the same block and were not permitted to cross the street alone due to our young age, made our friendship that much more special. I was no longer just conveniently there, I was chosen. I was wanted. There were numerous times when I would phone Ryan's house, back in the days before cell phones existed and phones were all attached to a wire that plugged into your wall. Sometimes he would be available, and sometimes he wouldn't, but the times when he was away from home doing something without me didn't matter, because there were also numerous times when our phone would ring, and it would actually be Ryan calling for me, choosing me over whatever other options he might have had. At least, it didn't matter for the first while. We were getting together on a regular basis at one another's homes, in the neighbourhood park, or along the dirt trails through the bushes abutting the nearby river. The occasional addition to these excursions of one of the other neighbourhood kids was even okay, because it gave me the opportunity to make known that I was not just Ryan's friend, but his best friend. As we explored the world around us, it seemed as if any differences we might have had were obscured by the discovery of a new bike path, the invention of a new game, or the wonders of a new realm of imagination. Even after that summer came to its inevitable close, Ryan and I remained friends, but as the school year progressed and our circle of friendship grew it became more and more apparent that for me, it was a circle of acquaintanceship. A part of me had assumed from the apparent evidence that having me as a friend was a special thing for Ryan as well, and perhaps it was. The problem with that assumption was that it ignored the possibility that I could be replaced so soon, so easily.

    I never actually lied about who my father was, claiming he was a policeman, a firefighter, or always overseas on some super secret spy mission. Even at that age I already knew from past experience that regardless of what I claimed about him, it would not change my standing in the social structure. It would have eventually become obvious to anyone that I was not following in the footsteps of any fantastic fictional father figure I could construct. I didn't share the shameful and embarrassing truth either, I simply told people that I didn't have a father and quietly waited for the subject to change. As tiresome as it was, I continued to strive for some semblance of acceptance by trying to prevent people's perceptions of me from forming based upon who I actually was, because who I was wasn't good enough. It turns out, being Ryan's best friend wasn't good enough either, especially once others began to vie for that position. As other kids expressed their interests and desires, mine and Ryan's diverged more and more. His world opened up to things like football and hockey, while I was more of an indoor person. There was still some overlap, and so for a time, I was able to hide my true self while trying to keep up with the crowd. I may actually owe, in part, the sense of dedication and perseverance I have today to my misguided stubborn efforts to continue showing up. To wait in the crowd as teams were picked, regardless of how much further to the end

I was chosen as time went on and my lack of talent became evident, until I was consistently last. To find that extra reserve of energy to continue through to the end of the day's sport, even when it seemed all of my strength was gone and all I could do was appear to be participating. To pay incredible attention to detail of the choreography of Vanilla Ice or MC Hammer's latest dance routine, and to pray that I could have a mind to rhyme and two hype feet.

Dedication and perseverance are wonderful tools to develop and use to propel yourself toward a goal, but they can only take you so far. They need to be renewed by the attainment of some result, or they begin to give way to hopelessness. For example, when I'm shovelling my long driveway after a blizzard, watching the ratio of freshly fallen snow versus freshly uncovered cement change in my favour helps me to persevere, to dedicate myself to completing the task. It's actually quite amazing how insignificant minus 30 degrees Celsius, even with an additional windchill factor, can seem in contrast to a sense of accomplishment. In contrast, having the audacity to try shovelling a driveway during a blizzard would not be likely to provide the same sense of accomplishment. When a lack of physical dexterity and agility makes your reality more of a mind to cry and two left feet, that's when you know this truly is a beat you can't touch. I may have developed a high tolerance for failure when I repeatedly stumbled over the latest dance moves, when the frequency with which I was passed a ball continued to decrease, and even as the team captains' words changed from "*I'll take Sean*" to "*looks like I get Sean*" and eventually to "*I guess we're stuck with Sean*". Tolerance can increase over time when exercised, but the problem with any human tolerance is that it has a limit.

A couple of years later, after yet another failure of mine to fit in, I overheard a schoolmate named Dennis telling Ryan, "*I tried giving him a chance, he's just not like us*". Dennis was, of course, speaking about me. As hurtful as this was at the time, it also shed light on the fact that Ryan had been standing up for me the whole time. He had not only been trying to include me, but had been encouraging others to do so as well. Having been completely unaware of that fact throughout those past years, it not only seemed as if Ryan's friendship was being stolen away from me, but also that he was intentionally favouring others over me. As the circumstances of life paraded along and the firelight fueled by my fury at being fatherless cast their shadowy images into my blurry view, I named them: hurt, betrayal, and abandonment.

Having held a job in a retail setting, and working my way into management, I've fielded my fair share of customer complaints. One of my favourites was the woman who wanted to return a pair of jeans because *"they fell apart the first time my son wore them!"* Never mind the glaring grass stains surrounding the holes that had mysteriously appeared at the knees. Obviously we were selling a substandard product. Whenever one of my employees was having a particularly bad day dealing with an unusually abundant amount of complaints, I would ask them how many customers they thought had come through our store in the past week. Inevitably, the number would be much higher than the count of those who had returned with some issue. My follow up question would be, *"do you ever return to a store to tell them you're satisfied with your purchase?"* This world has a tendency to put negatives directly in our view, obscuring the good results which could be feeding our dedication and perseverance. Many of us, and especially those of us accustomed to hurt, betrayal, and abandonment, choose to focus on the negative even when we're surrounded by good.

Even Jesus was called a liar: *"Among the crowds there was widespread whispering about him. Some said, 'He is a good man.' Others replied, 'No, he deceives the people.'"* (John 7:12) This was only a short time after Jesus took five loaves of bread and two fish, and used them to miraculously feed a crowd of 5,000 men, along with unnumbered women and children. I have no idea where these people think this alleged fraud was hiding all of that bread and fish out on that hill in the wilderness, but they were certainly not focussing on the good. Similarly, I was not focussing on the good that was in my life at the time. Even though Ryan had other friends, I was still his friend. Even though I was not close with these other friends, I was often included, even if it was begrudgingly. Even though I was poor at sports and the like, I was great in the classroom. Even though I really didn't belong amid the crowd with which Ryan was spending more and more time, there were other groups I could have belonged in, but missed out on due to the blinders I was wearing. Not literal blinders, I wasn't *that* weird as a kid. I kept on trying to fit my square peg into a round hole, trying to hold on to what I thought was good in my life, until one day the frustration culminated in a fit worthy of a toddler throwing their Playskool workbench across the room.

I don't actually recall exactly what happened that day at school, but I do know that my immature, damaged mind filed it into the already overflowing drawer of my heart where all of the other apparent hurts, betrayals, and abandonments were kept. Whatever it was that led to the fight with Ryan, it was the proverbial straw that broke the camel's back. I do remember that when the bell rang out to signal the end of recess, this time I knew that the day was not over and I was not supposed to go home yet. I decided I was going home anyway, because even if I could manage to get my sobbing under control, I couldn't bear to return to class and show my tear covered face. Doing so would only perpetuate my pain, and my peers' perception that the kid without a father was completely unable to "man up". This time, I had no pride in myself for making it home, only shame about the fact that all I could do was run away and hide. I was now old enough to have been entrusted with my own key to our home, and so at least there was no trepidation about what would occur when I reached the door this time. However, my expectations were once again proven false, because when I let myself in, even though it was the middle of a workday for her, my mother was at home and had been roused by the sound of the front door opening. She asked once again, *"what are you doing at home?"*

Once I had told her my story, and after whatever length of time it took me to once again calm down in her embrace, it finally occurred to me that she shouldn't even be there. She ought to have been out delivering packages, because at this point in time she was a driver for a local courier company. It turns out that in the course of driving her route, my mother had been stopped at the same intersection of her current boyfriend who happened to also be a courier. She had honked, and waved, and tried to get his attention to no avail. In her mind, he had ignored her, even though reality was likely something different. She had been hurt, and had potentially also felt betrayed and abandoned. After telling me this story, my mother capped it off with, *"that's alright though, we don't need anyone else anyway"*.

Those words were intended as a source of comfort. They were meant to instill strength and self confidence. My mother was trying to teach me a good thing, that our worth does not come from other people, and she was right. I took it the wrong way, and used it as the foundation upon which I began to build walls around my heart. It wasn't a decision that I made at that point in time, or at any point in time for that matter. I never thought, *"that's a wonderful piece of advice, upon which I'm going to predicate every relationship from now on"*. Her comforting phrase, though intended for good, was a slow poison. It echoed through the empty canyon of my soul, over and over. Yet, that lie was unlike an echo in that it never seemed to fade regardless of the passage of time, but perpetually repeated almost in spite of time itself, as if to say, *"you don't heal all wounds, time, you can't heal me"*.

I did make a conscious decision later that afternoon to act upon the day's events, when I actually wrote myself a note which read, *"don't talk to Ryan, he's a jerk"*. Except, I used a different word than "jerk". For some time after, I carried that note in my pocket each day, because some part of me knew that I was likely to forgive as the memory of his alleged transgression faded from mind. My stubbornness was not yet fully grown though, and so as that scrap of paper became more and more worn and tattered, so did any argument or excuse that I had for shunning my once best friend. Never mind the fact that by avoiding Ryan I was isolating myself, unable to attempt belonging to the wider group anymore, as he would always be a fixture within. I also did not have the courage to approach any other group, especially as it seemed the cliques had formed, and none were accepting new applications. Cutting ourselves off from community, as tempting as it may be as a defense mechanism, only leads to more pain. A fortress of solitude is especially lonely when it's metaphorical, and we're surrounded by opportunities to take another chance at belonging. My tolerance for that loneliness was soon exceeded by my yearning for acceptance and belonging. Just as I don't recall the exact scenario which led to this whole mess, I also don't recall any tangible steps Ryan and I took toward reconciliation. I simply know that one day, I scrapped that scrap of paper, and by the next day, we were friends again.

There is something special about children's acceptance of one another. Somewhere along the line, we begin to hold grudges. We deny our nagging conscience telling us to forgive until that voice fades away, giving in to our prideful insistence that its admonishments are baseless. The truth that we know in our hearts becomes stifled by pride, or even by a desire for vengeance which overtakes our desire for love. That original truth, that we are meant to love and to be loved, might become obscured but never does leave our hearts. That truth was there from the beginning, and as children we were so much more in tune with it. Even though I tried to hold a grudge against Ryan, I couldn't. Even though I must have actually hurt and confused him for a time while I was avoiding him, and he might have even felt betrayed or abandoned by me, we reconciled. There was no mediation, no negotiation, no peace treaty or armistice. There was simply a couple of boys who had a few things in common and wanted to spend time together. We were children motivated not by pride nor vengeance, but by a brotherly love for one another.

One day some parents were trying to get their children through some crowds to see Jesus, but some of Jesus' close followers scolded them for trying to bother Him. Maybe they thought it was Jesus' day off and that He had earned some rest, but nonetheless, *"Jesus called the children to him and said, 'Let the little children come to me, and do not hinder them, for the kingdom of God belongs to such as these. Truly I tell you, anyone who will not receive the kingdom of God like a little child will never enter it."* (Luke 18:16-17). I think that we had much more faith in one another when we were children, and that if we can drop the pretenses and walls we've built, if we can expunge the slow poisons we've ingested, we can get back to the truth which was there at the beginning. No matter how many times we've moved, how far we've veered off course, or how out of sight our intended destination may be, there is a person inside each one of us who is *"like these children"*.

Furthermore, *"In the beginning was the Word, and the Word was with God, and the Word was God. He was with God in the beginning. Through Him all things were made; without Him nothing was made that has been made. In Him was life, and that life was the light of all mankind. The light shines in the darkness, and the darkness has not overcome it."* (John 1:1-5) This capital 'W' Word who John speaks of is Jesus; the same Jesus who is never too weary to spend time with the children. The same Jesus who encourages us to have faith to receive the Kingdom of God like children. Jesus, through whom everything was created, and have you ever created something that you didn't intend to keep? If it didn't turn out quite the way you wanted, wouldn't you take delight in your creation anyway, and perhaps even try to remove any blemishes? Even if you've given up on a project, how much more dedication and perseverance does God have for His creation than any human ever could? His life *"was the light of ALL mankind"*, regardless of blemish. It's tempting to say that God has limitless tolerance, but that is not quite right. He does not simply tolerate us, he forgives us and yearns for us to come to Him as His children. Ryan and I did not reconcile by simply beginning to tolerate one another, we completely let go of whatever prior transgressions there were, to the point where they are no longer a part of memory. That childlike forgiveness is a mere glimpse into the forgiveness Jesus gives. There is no circumstantial imposition of God's dedication and perseverance toward redeeming us, to His love for us. He certainly has no lack of options, and yet, we are chosen. We are wanted.

Though I know these things now, it wasn't until quite a few moves later when I finally made it all the way out of my dark cave and chose to step into that light which had been there all along. One of the things God gave us is the ability to choose, and as long as we have that ability, it seems that darkness also has the dedication and perseverance to vie for our attention.

A Hero(?) Is Born

"Just turn around, love will find you." – Paul Brandt

I began to gasp for breath the moment the edge of the desk collided with my ribcage. I had felt physical pain many times before, but this is the first time I remember being so completely winded that for a while, I wondered whether I would ever recover. The desk had actually been a table, which I would estimate to have measured about two and a half by six feet, but we referred to them as desks in science class because this was where we all sat, two kids per table. Except of course, I had one to myself. We were at an age where "teen" was beginning to appear in our number of years, and so there was no shortage of angst, discord, and even outright rivalry between many of my peers. This was one game for which I was never chosen last, it was actually quite the opposite. Though I had not completely given up on being accepted, there were some instances where my dedication and perseverance toward that end had reached their limit through repeated failure to see any semblance of success. Dennis was one such instance, and so when he took the seat in front of me and began his usual tirade about every little thing that was wrong with me, I responded. I had nothing to lose, and had not yet realized the wisdom to know that responding also offered me nothing to gain. One of the few benefits, if you can call it that, of having two older brothers at this point in life was that I was privy to some rather scathing, cutting edge insults. It seemed that my particular choice of retort this day was quite shocking not only to Dennis, but to the entire classroom who, by no accident on my part, heard exactly what I had to say about him. In that exact moment, I counted myself lucky that our teacher had not yet arrived for class such that he would have heard those words from my mouth. In the next moment, my luck immediately ran out as Dennis rammed that table backward in retribution for our classmates' laughter being redirected at him.

The spots which had formed a black cloud in my vision dissipated as I heard Dennis braying, "*ha -ha, he can't breathe!*" I began instead to see red, and as I somehow managed to lift myself from my chair, he must have seen something as well, because Dennis also stood, hands out before himself in that classic warding gesture as he began to retreat, away from me. I practically ran at him and barked, "*I'll show you who can't breathe!*" as my hands shot around his neck and my momentum propelled him with surprising force against the blackboard at the front of the room. After a time, times, or half a time, the luck that had already turned bad became worse. Rather, from a proper perspective, my luck soon improved when, as if in response to some siren only he could hear ringing out, our teacher arrived for class in time to witness Dennis' bulging eyes as his face began to transition from red to purple. Mr. Arnason promptly pulled my hands apart from Dennis' neck, ushered me directly out of the room, and all of the way to the principal's office.

I was no stranger to being chastised for my behaviour, and so even though this particular disciplinary discussion was more serious than most due to the violent nature of my actions, I listened just as well as I normally did. That is, not well at all. It's safe to assume there were things said such as "*what were you thinking?*", "*violence doesn't solve anything*", "*I'm disappointed in you*", and many more of those tired old adult sayings which I'm sure I've repeated to people younger than me in my more recent years. I had heard them all before, and their impact became less and less meaningful each time. Sometimes when we're tuned out of a conversation, something does suddenly seem significant enough to snap our attention back to the speaker, and this turned out to be just such a time. The atmosphere of the room completely changed, and I think the principal felt it as well, because he finally stopped speaking when he saw my reaction to his statement, "*You could have killed him*".

A near decade's worth of feelings began seeping, no, pouring from my heart at once. Whatever recesses into which I had been stuffing them like some kind of hoarder instead of just processing them and then letting them go, those places could hold no more. The bundles of old newspapers with headlines such as "*Weakling is picked last again!*" or "*Loser sets a new record for most days sitting alone at lunch!*" came unfurled and whirled across my field of vision. The strange keepsakes that were piled about, things like a dented up die cast car, a torn Archie comic book, or even a five dollar bill with "STOLEN" stamped across the front were overturned, scattered, and lifted to cast shadows over me. The cockroaches were disturbed by this environmental shift, and they began to scutter about my brain, the sound of each one sending out a sickening accusatory whisper:

"*useless!*"

"*liar!*"

"*thief!*"

"*ugly!*"

"*trash!*"

"*unloved!*"

As memory after memory and hurt after hurt were uncovered, slowly the foundation of it all came into view. Underneath every mask I had ever worn, below every behaviour I had adopted out of a need for acceptance, behind the belief that I should be full of shame, there was the reason for it all. The alleged truth of my identity, the rotten, festering wound I had been trying to heal by pretending it wasn't there was not simply reopened, but was widened by that statement *"you could have killed him"*. The stigmatic lie which some unknown malevolent force seemed to have been nurturing inside of me burst forth from the depths of my subconscious mind into a new realm of awareness. Out of a chasm so deep that I could have previously only suspected what lay within, there emerged a hideous understanding: the thing that was in my father was also in me.

In the books of 1 Kings and 2 Kings in the Old Testament, we read of the events surrounding the passing of the kingdom of Israel from one monarch to the next. Though at times the kingdom was taken by force, the custom at the time was that upon the death of a king, generally his son would take the throne. There are many such transitions where, in spite of the king having been a godly man, his successor turns away from the good his father had done and leads the nation into idol worship and all other sorts of debauchery and evil. On the flipside, there are also many such transitions where, in spite of the king having been an evil man, his successor does his best to undo the damage, to right the wrongs, to repent and atone, to lead Israel back to God. Oftentimes throughout, we hear of a prophet, a man of God, a spiritual guide who encourages the kings to either perpetuate the good of their father, or to turn from their evil ways. *"Although the Lord sent prophets to the people to bring them back to him, and though they testified against them, they would not listen."* (2 Chronicles 24:19). In the verses which follow those words we hear about some of the ways in which the people are led to disobey God, to disregard His forgiveness, love, and security. Another nation, Assyria, had invaded the land and shackled the citizens. In spite of a clear history of God giving Israel victory over armies much larger than their own during times when they were committed to Him, for some reason they seemed to believe, as many of us do in our struggles, *"that can't happen for us today"*.

At the same time the Israelites were exiled from their land by Assyria, there was a king by the name of Hezekiah ruling over Israel's sister kingdom, Judah. Hezekiah's father, Ahaz, *"did not do what was right in the eyes of the Lord his God. He followed the ways of the kings of Israel and even sacrificed his son in the fire"* (2 Kings 16:2-3). Obviously, this was a different son, and obviously, having a father who is a murderer can set a person on a destructive path. Yet, Hezekiah *"did what was right in the eyes of the Lord"* (2 Kings 18:3), and *"Hezekiah trusted in the Lord, the God of Israel. There was no one like him among all the kings of Judah, either before him or after him."* (2 Kings 18:5). It would seem that regardless of a father's actions, perhaps even in spite of a person's upbringing, we can shake off the shackles of shame, and under the shepherding of our saviour God can live a life not of ill repute, but of renown.

I'm not going to say that the principal of my junior high school was a prophet. I do not recall him ever speaking a single word about God, even though back in those days God had not yet been banned from the public education system. I also don't believe that he had any idea about my father, and so I cannot say that his poignant warning had purposefully been so personal. Regardless, something in me had been exposed. Whether or not by divine intervention or inspiration, his insinuation of the darkness dwelling within me directed my attention to the diverging paths before me. I had stumbled along my rocky road, first carrying and then dragging the burden of me, struggling more and more as the weight of my shame steadily increased. Not knowing where this road would lead nor how far I had to go, I was simply striving to remain within its boundaries because I had no concept of the freedom which might lie in the pastures on either side. As I looked up from my feet, both the metaphorical pair on that road and the physical pair upon which I had affixed my gaze while awaiting the end of my most recent lecture, here before me was a crossroads. Here was a warning, and an opportunity. Here was a conviction. Or was it a condemnation?

From around 140 A.D. there is a Greek text known as The Shepherd of Hermas, which references the idea that *"There are two angels with a man – one of righteousness, and the other of iniquity"*. The first time I was introduced to this concept was through an episode of The Flintstones, when Fred had an angel version of himself on one shoulder, and a devil version on the other. These two mini-Freds in their respective costumes would each speak to him, trying to influence his behaviour. The angel tried to guide Fred toward love, peace, patience, and kindness. The devil aimed for actions which led to indifference, discord, anger, and strife. The writer of the episode seemed to want to teach us through Fred's initial capitulation to the devil that there are consequences to selfishness. Subsequently, when Fred finally gave that devil the boot and began to listen to the angel, the moral of the story was that forgiveness and restoration are available for those who turn from their evil ways, repent, and do good. This lesson certainly ought to have already resided somewhere in my mind when I was brought to this particular crossroads. Whether through conscience or through spiritual influence, we intrinsically know the difference between right and wrong. *"For since the creation of the world God's invisible qualities – his eternal power and divine nature – have been clearly seen, being understood from what has been made, so that people are without excuse"* (Romans 1:20). I had no excuse. The signposts at my crossroads were as clear as the notions that grass was green and the sky was blue. Like Hezekiah, I could choose a better path than that of my father. I could heed this warning, take the opportunity which this new awareness had presented, and become a better man than my father had ever been!

It was not long until the time came for the mandatory apology to Dennis. Regardless of the fact that this was a rite which adults force children to perform any time one has wronged another, I put legitimate effort into expressing my remorse. I knew that simply reciting empty words was no way to start out on a new path. In the presence of the school principal, the apology was accepted as it normally is in these scenarios, I suppose because Dennis wanted to move on from the situation just as much as I did. Perhaps more so, considering the weak, unathletic, insignificant loser had somehow physically overpowered him. Regardless of the exact reason, that was the second last thing I ever heard out of him, because he steered clear of me from then on. The last was to overhear him tell a certain former best friend of mine who I was beginning to see less and less, "*I tried to give him a chance, he's just not like us*".

I tried to keep a low profile over the next few days, but as I'm sure you know, notoriety for our misdeeds is much easier to come by than renown for the good. This seemed especially true for me in junior high school, when for some time after my violent outburst I was unable to enter a room or even walk down the hall without noticing sideways glances, whispers, or even the occasional redirection of someone's path as if in an effort to avoid me. It didn't seem to matter, if it even occurred to me at the time, that these behaviours were nothing new. I should have been accustomed to the averted gaze of kids who didn't want to make eye contact, lest the nerd take it as an invitation to say hello. I had already heard enough rude comments and insults about myself which may or may not have been intended as private conversation. I certainly wasn't a stranger to being avoided or ignored, either. In the wake of what I had done though, these behaviours became more prolific in my view, and the logical assumption was to draw a correlation between the two.

Of course, I wasn't the only one in the entire school who felt like an outcast. There were others who could only dream of treating a bully the way I had, and as my fifteen minutes of fame faded away alongside any hope I still might have held about belonging with the cool crowd, it was with these other denizens of obscurity where I found some modicum of acceptance, and even admiration. A couple of these other kids had been peripheral acquaintances for some time. These were the kids who, like me, often ended up alone on the playground, in the lunchroom, or most dangerous of all because of the relative lack of supervision, walking home from school. There is truth to that old adage 'birds of a feather flock together', as evidenced by the fact that we had repeatedly ended up hanging around each other, perhaps out of a belief that there was safety in numbers. As it seemed the door was shutting on any opportunity for me to continue pursuing belonging in the one crowd, the door was opening for 'hanging around each other' to turn into 'hanging out with one another' for myself and these other outsiders. Though we never named our group like the main cast of Stephen King's "It" did, for all intents and purposes we were just as much of a "Loser's Club" as those clown murdering children.

If I was truly going to choose a new path, to correct my flight plan, then something had to change, and a new peer group seemed like a good place to start. It actually wasn't long before my clean slate began to fill with the lines of a new story. The more time I spent avoiding the crowd I had previously gravitated toward, the more I encountered those who were also avoiding that crowd. As lunch breaks became less lonely, and as spare periods were spent in the library or the computer lab instead of the sidelines of a basketball court or football field, it seemed I was finally finding some belonging on a path which was more congruent with my true self. The problem with comfort and trust is that if you let your guard down with the wrong people, you open yourself up to influences which can be difficult to resist. It can be especially easy to let your guard down when, for the very first time, you finally find the acceptance you had always wanted. Although it was evident that the path I had been on was not good, and that I needed a new direction, it does not automatically follow that the next path I chose was good. It turned out that the same reason for this change would also become the catalyst leading to the formation of a new identity.

My Loser's Club never seemed to have a shortage of bullies, but for the most part they were handled through either avoidance or tattling. Every once in a while, there comes a situation which must be met head on, and as the one member of our troupe who had experience fighting back, it only seemed logical for that task to fall to me. In retrospect, it was not wise for us to have chosen a table in the cafeteria right next to the cool kids that one day, but alas, there we were, in the line of fire of their ketchup packets. Apparently, being "cool" meant that you threw things at those with lesser social status and physical stature whenever the opportunity arose. Could we have avoided or removed ourselves from this situation? Of course. Could we have reported this behaviour to an adult and chanced later repercussions? Absolutely. Would it be a good idea to instead hold our ground and return fire? Definitely not. So, that is exactly what we did, and whether by some miracle or by some cruel twist of fate, for the first time in my life, I was able to guide a projectile with such pinpoint accuracy that it landed directly between the eyes of the leader of the bullies, splattering ketchup across his face. Or, perhaps it was catsup. Either way, it was enough to end this battle. Not because I had struck some decisive blow which allowed our side to claim victory, but because it was now time to escalate matters. When Bluto slowly stood and began to head in my direction, I wish I could tell you that I simply popped an entire can of spinach into my mouth, swallowed it in one bite, and defended the honour of my Loser's Club with one uppercut, but unfortunately I did not have a can opener handy at the time. As a side note, this boy's name was not Bluto, but I cannot recall his name, so it might as well have been considering his girth. As he lumbered my way, I did what I knew to do; I ran. I ran out of that cafeteria, down the hallway, and up the nearest set of stairs in view out of some hope that this neanderthal would believe I was cornering myself on the second floor. I then outright sprinted across to the furthest stairs back down, then outside and amidst a large group of kids lounging around in the grassy area where I could potentially blend in. Finding myself gasping for breath as the result of yet another incident, I considered my options.

As I was wracking my brain for a solution, the school bell rang out signalling the end of the lunch period. The throng of students within which I had been camouflaging myself began to dissipate, and so I stood and slowly made my way inside, toward my locker to retrieve the books necessary for my next class. Considering Bluto was a grade or two ahead of me, it seemed that continuing with my daily routine ought to be a safe enough course of action, but the problem with routines is that they are predictable, especially by those who know you. At my locker awaiting my arrival was my friend Erik, who had been present for the Great Ketchup Battle. He barely finished saying, *"thank you for standing up for us. I'm sorry, they made me show them where to find you"* when Bluto came around the nearby corner. Any hope I had of escaping in the opposite direction immediately disappeared as I realized his cronies were coming from the opposite direction. My retreat had been cut off; I had foolishly been caught in a basic pincer maneuver. As they closed in, I knew my fate was sealed as all of the other kids filed off to their next scene, like oblivious movie extras who never come to the aid of the protagonist in times of need. This was the moment in time when I would either have to realize some previously unknown potential, to tap into the mutant superpowers which had lay dormant within me until this moment of dire need, or I would have to take my beating, hopefully like a man. This time it was my turn to raise my hands in that classic warding gesture, and to my dismay there was no resultant laser beam, no spider's webbing, no telekinetic wave of energy to push away my foes, not even so much as a sparkle.

To my surprise, Bluto did not immediately begin pummelling me for my transgression, though it may have been better in the long run if he had. He looked over my shoulder at my open locker door, grinned like that idiot hyena Ed in the Lion King, and barked, "*I know what happens to me later if you get a beating. I'll make you a deal that saves us both some trouble.*" Pointing at my locker, he continued, "*get in, and I won't touch you.*" I hesitated for only a moment, but that was apparently enough for Bluto's cronies to lose patience and make the decision for me. One pushed me backwards and crammed me into the small space as the other closed the door, and I immediately heard the click of the lock being snapped into place.

I learned later that Erik had been forbidden from opening the door, and it became easy to forgive him for making decisions which would save him from the same fate which had befallen me. While still in my imprisonment though, I felt my familiar old friends, Betrayal and Abandonment, somehow managing to squeeze into this tiny space along with me. Looking back, or looking in from an outside perspective, it may seem overly dramatic to say I could relate to the words: "*I am overwhelmed with troubles and my life draws near to death. I am counted among those who go down to the pit; I am like one without strength. I am set apart with the dead, like the slain who lie in the grave, whom you remember no more, who are cut off from your care.*" (Psalm 88:3-5) From my contorted point of view, not only physically but also mentally and emotionally, I might as well have fallen into a pit and died. Any hope I had at fitting in with anyone was gone; when people heard of this disgrace, I would be a social leper.

I'm uncertain how long I waited before I deemed it safe to begin pounding on the locker door without alerting the Bluto Brigade to my attempts at liberation. I know my fists weren't hammering as frantically as one might imagine, instead beating out at a steady pace using as little strength as possible with each strike so as to prolong my ability to call attention to my predicament. When I eventually heard "*what's all this racket?!*" from nearby in that unique yet vague somewhere-from-Europe accent which identified the school's head custodian, I thanked God not only for a saviour, but also that it was not another student. In between sobs, I somehow managed to relay the combination through the steel door, and was soon freed. I refused to say how I had ended up in that locker, or who else might have been involved, because as we all know, snitches get stitches. I simply grabbed my jacket and left, not only the scene of my most recent shameful indignity, but following my pattern I left the school. Regardless of what the clock or my class schedule may have said, it was time to go home for the day. A wise person once said not to worry about tomorrow, for today has enough trouble of its own. Whatever consequences there would be for skipping out on my afternoon classes could be excused when I gave my explanation. I was much more concerned with the shame which would be heaped upon me by my peers, and delaying that for as long as possible was my single goal at that moment.

As seems to have been the pattern throughout all of my years, the next day did inevitably arrive. At some point in time, Jesus will return and ultimately end this pattern, *"but about that day or hour no one knows, not even the angels in Heaven, nor the Son, but only the Father"* (Matthew 24:36). I can therefore tell you with a rather high level of confidence that whatever you might be dreading about tomorrow, you'll likely have to face. I know that when I think back to times I've been dreading a situation, I had built it up in my mind to something much bigger than it turned out to be, and I bet that if you think back, you'll see the same thing has happened in your life, and you got through. I also know that I was practically crippled with fear the morning after the locker incident, yet somehow even then I knew that avoiding the pain of embarrassment and shame was only compounding that fear. Somehow, I made it through my morning routine, got myself to school on time, and as I sheepishly approached my Loser's Club in our usual morning meet-up spot, they all picked up handfuls of rocks and stoned me to death. I know, you're thinking that I don't sound very dead. Well, I got better. OK, so in reality, when I sheepishly approached my Loser's Club that morning, they fell silent at my arrival, began to cast sideways glances at one another, and then, one by one, began to applaud. One of them put his arm around my shoulders and said, *"thanks for taking one for the team, Locker Boy"*.

We may never see "Locker Boy: the Bluto Battle" in theaters, but it seemed that my act of defiance, my decision to meet wrong with wrong, regardless of how it had turned out, had somehow earned me some kind of anti-hero status. Having earned this newfound respect, it seemed to me that I had found a new path. I didn't need to continue chasing after the dream of being allowed into a certain peer group. I no longer had reason to try to be someone I was not out of some misguided hope that it would result in belonging. I was able to be myself, as disobedient, rebellious, and angry as that self may have been, and not only belong within this group, but stand out from it. What was not obvious to me at the time, perhaps because I had not yet come by any knowledge of a man like Hezekiah, was that this was not a turning point setting me upon the right path. This was not a correction in my flight plan. This was an over-correction, redirecting me from one perilous destination to another.

Balancing The Books

"The right to be irresponsible and stupid is something I hold very dear. And luckily it is something I do well." – Bono

When a desire for acceptance is one of the largest motivational forces in your life, you may find yourself accepting whatever acceptance you are given, and molding yourself in the image of what you see others accepting. This is one of the reasons gangs are successful in recruiting youth into their ranks, with promises not only of glory and riches, but of a kind of pseudo-family. It's a shadow version of what family is intended to be, where more often than not you will be betrayed or abandoned by someone watching out for themselves first. I realize this sounds very much like an actual family to many people, because as I've mentioned I've felt both betrayal and abandonment from my own family. That is just one more reason why so many accept this shadow version of family, because it can also have that sense of familiarity which, regardless of its dysfunction, is comforting.

When Moses was leading the nation of Israel out of their captivity and through the desert, they experienced the same dysfunctional desire to return to the relative comfort of what they had known. When they looked back at how difficult the first part of their journey had already been, and imagined how difficult it could be to continue through the desert, they threw a temper tantrum and yelled at Moses, claiming that at least they had food back in Egypt. So what if they were fed barely enough to continue living and to have just enough strength to perform forced labor. Getting beaten for not meeting your quota wasn't really that bad, as long as there were scraps to feed on at the end of another long day in slavery. Also, it was nice to feel needed. The Israelites wanted the quick fix, and in absence of the promise given to them not immediately materializing, their hope for the future was quickly overrun by fear of the unknown.

Just because many actual families consistently fail to live up to a benchmark of love and acceptance, it does not mean the standard does not exist. We humans are created with hope as a default setting, and in our hope for a certain standard or even for an ideal, we often go looking for love in all the wrong places. I was personally never recruited to a gang, likely due to my affinity for country music and distaste for rap and hip hop. Had the opportunity arisen though, I do wonder sometimes exactly how much further I might have gone out of hope for acceptance.

While I was still in high school, my family moved to yet another new neighbourhood, far enough away from where we had lived that I would be going to a new school full of completely unfamiliar faces. Any respect and admiration I had been able to earn from my old Loser's Club in the wake of the Bluto Battle and subsequent escapades would expire. All of the energy spent fighting back against those who had me pegged as an easy target, and the times when I would even instigate the fight which I saw as inevitable, all of that social credit was now null and void. Perhaps having a fresh start thrust upon was a blessing in disguise, but I certainly did not see beyond this veil. Much like the majority of Moses' spies who first reported back about their Promised Land, I was blinded to the possibility of any blessing which may have been before me by the overwhelming fear of the occupants of this new territory.

One of my first lessons in this new school came not from the classroom, but during that familiar lunchtime gathering where a much larger, more intimidating crowd was present. I quickly learned how DJ Tanner, a character from the popular television show "Full House", felt on her first day of high school. I didn't show up in the exact same outfit as a teacher like she did, but I was ridiculed based solely upon my appearance nonetheless. DJ retreated to a phone booth to pretend she was calling a friend at a different school during her lunch break, while I simply retreated to any place I could find with the fewest people, preferably zero. There was no way I was going to start this new school year in the line of fire of ketchup packets, catsup packets, rubber bands, or spitballs. For those of you who aren't old enough to remember things like when the internet was invented, a "phone booth" was a plexiglass enclosure, usually about four feet wide and long, maybe seven feet high, with a closing door. It had a wired land-line phone which would allow you to place a local call for 25 cents. Oh, and a "land-line", well, just get off my lawn and go google it. The important thing to note is that even in this new environment, even with another summers' worth of growth under my belt, it was not long until I once again received the message, *"don't even try to fit in anywhere or make friends, because you can't"*. Of course, I had not only developed a distaste for being told I can't do something, but I had also learned that there was one way I could fit in. All I had to do was await the right opportunity.

I did eventually fall in with a small group of misfits, schoolmates who like me, also didn't quite fit into any of the usual popular cliques, or the unpopular ones for that matter. We really didn't have much in common, other than the fact that we had nothing in common with most everyone else. The mutual acceptance of one another's acceptance was "good enough" in the absence of anything that was good, or enough. We were able to camouflage ourselves from the other packs by becoming a flock of our own, in the hopes of no longer being singled out. Looking back, I can see now that we were never friends. We were acquaintances through circumstance, which was becoming a common theme in my life. We rarely spent time with each other outside of school, we never spoke of anything beyond shallow conversation, and some part of each of us might have even been embarrassed by one another. Some underlying, unspoken understanding existed though; that as each of us might try to be accepted by the "cool" kids, those of us whose attempts to do so failed would always be welcomed back within the safety net which we were for one another.

The whispers that had been in my mind from early childhood, those which had told me that I couldn't be accepted by anyone, that I had nothing to give, that I was of no use and that I provided no benefit in relationship with others, they all began to clamour for attention. My own subconscious assumptions about myself which I had based upon my previous experiences told me that if I were ever going to be accepted by others, I had to become something other than myself. In an environment where the things I enjoyed, such as reading, crossword puzzles, logic puzzles, or various other intellectual pastimes resulted in undesirable labels such as geek or nerd, I believed that I was better off hiding that part of myself in order to survive through another day. Simply surviving was no longer enough though, not after my brief stint as an anti-hero. There had to be a way that I might stand out from my flock and, for at least a little while, enjoy life as a sheep in wolf's clothing.

Realizing that the other kids in high school seemed to want to be around those who were more athletic, or who always dressed in the trendy clothes, or sometimes, those who would make themselves appear better than others by bullying them, I tried in various ways to re-form myself into a portrayal of something similar. Unable to control how others viewed the characteristics which were natural to me, I took control of which characteristics in me they were allowed to see. I told those whispers in my mind that they can't tell me what I can't do; I can be something that someone will accept, or possibly even admire. It had happened once, and so it could happen again. I just wasn't willing to go to the extreme of walking up to the biggest guy in the yard and punching him in the face. This wasn't a literal prison where, if we believe television, such displays of bravery are supposed to garner instant respect. Mine was an internal incarceration.

As is all too often the case, an opportunity to do the wrong thing for what seemed to be the right reason soon presented itself. I don't know what it is about school cafeterias. It might have something to do with all of those teenage hormones being crammed into one room, jostling against one another at crowded tables. Perhaps the protein refuelling our energy reserves was an encouragement to immediately burn some off. Maybe it was the relative lack of supervision where the adult to student ratio was perpetually imbalanced in favour of us getting away with shenanigans; and if you shenan once, you'll probably shenan-again. Likely it was some combination of these and other factors, many of which would have been my own mental and emotional issues, which created the perfect storm to capsize any sense of homeostasis I may have been experiencing.

When Jane, one of the girls who were surprisingly part of our group, sat at the table and rolled up her sleeves, I don't recall who it was that asked where the bruises on her arm had come from. I know that it wasn't me, because even though she was one of the outcasts, one of the leftover people who didn't fit anywhere else just like the rest of us, she was still a girl. There was no attraction and therefore no fear of rejection from any kind of romantic standpoint, but still, there was that strange awkwardness inside of me that acted as a barrier to communication with the other gender. At least, there was until Jane answered, *"one of the guys in class this morning was grabbing me really hard, to keep me from going to rat him out for hitting me"*. This sounded like a job for Locker Boy.

"Who was it? If he's in the cafeteria right now, point him out" was my immediate response. I'm not certain what it was about my voice at that moment, but time seemed to have completely stopped for everyone at our table. Lunch was forgotten, not a word was uttered, not an itch was scratched. All eyes were like those at a tennis match, bouncing from me to Jane, from Jane to me. She broke the silence with a name, a description, and after a look around the room, a location. Once again, in spite of the existence of a myriad of better options, I allowed my indignation to get the best of me. I would later justify my actions by portraying myself as the proverbial judge, jury, and executioner; the one standing up for what was right versus a boy who had committed an unforgivable sin. He had hit a girl. In the moment, of course I was not considering these justifications, or anything else for that matter. I went on auto-pilot. Even if I had pre-emptively thought out the course of action that I did take and justified myself beforehand, I did not know then what I know now, something which is a defining characteristic of an anti-hero. If our actions need justification, then they're probably unjust.

I know that I am forgiven, and have since forgiven myself for what followed, but not anytime soon after. I felt neither guilt nor shame for my actions until much later, which some people might tell you is a good thing. It absolutely is good to not be ashamed of who you are, but I daresay that I should have been ashamed of what I did. Today's culture has reduced guilt, shame, and any other bad feeling to an emotional health issue which needs to be addressed through self-help books, therapy, and pills, which only address the symptomatic feelings. I've gleaned wisdom from self-help books. I've garnered insight from counsellors. I know people who are much more stable and productive when taking their prescribed medication. These things are not bad, they're simply not enough. That is why some people will escalate their attempts to feel better, or skip over those things entirely, turning to other alternatives in an effort to forget, even temporarily, that life is not always what we want it to be. There is an addiction for every taste, for every personality: drugs, alcohol, work, sex, relationships, television, food, porn, sports, adrenaline highs, and so many more. I've actually met a person who was addicted to attending recovery groups. I think that feeling bad sometimes can be a good thing, in the same way that warning lights on your car's dashboard are a good thing. Feeling guilty? Check your behaviours and determine whether you need to seek forgiveness. Feeling shame? Check your heart and realize that doing bad things does not mean you are a bad person. Feeling hungry? Eat. Don't remain in the state that is setting off warning lights, or things will end up worse. Just accept that these warnings exist for a reason, and require a reaction.

Guilt and shame are present in our lives to convict us, not to condemn us. Conviction is the realization of wrongdoing which sets us upon the path to atonement. Condemnation is the accusation of wrong-*being* which sets us upon the path to misery, self-loathing, and apathy. Conviction says, *"you failed, do better next time"*. Condemnation says, *"you're a failure, give up"*. Our Father God never gives up on us; "*...there is now no condemnation for those who are in Christ Jesus*" (Romans 8:1), and He wants better for us: "*Fools make fun of guilt, but the godly acknowledge it and seek reconciliation*" (Proverbs 14:9, NLT). If you find yourself experiencing guilt or shame, that means you have a conscience. Some people might say it's that angel on your shoulder; while the devil is trying to condemn you, the angel is trying to redeem you. Still others would say it's God's Holy Spirit whispering truths to you about the person you're capable of becoming on the other side of an apology, directing you toward your Hezekiah moment.

If there was any semblance of conscience, angel, or Holy Spirit speaking to me as I rose from that cafeteria table, I certainly did not listen. I would not have recognized fatherly guidance if I had heard it. I wove around tables toward my destination, eyes fixed upon my target, anger swelling and propelling me the entire way. When I stopped at his side, this putrid being, this perpetrator of such a vile act had barely turned his face in my direction before my fist collided with one side of his head with such force that the other was propelled in an arc toward the table, where it almost comically smashed his plate of gravy covered fries before thudding against the wood surface underneath. As he straightened back up, I know he heard me at least through the one ear which had not been filled with mushy potato when I growled, "*you don't ever hit a girl, or there's worse than that coming for you*", because he swore it would never happen again. Also, whether from the physical pain, the tone of my voice, or the words I actually used which were censored into the paraphrase I've provided, something else happened. He began to cry, and I ought to have been ashamed that seeing his tears gave me great satisfaction. Instead I felt smug, and even righteous for a few moments, until a hand fell upon my shoulder from behind, and I turned to realize that the adult to student ratio in the cafeteria that day had not been low enough to work in my favour. Before I could be told what to do, I asked, *"principal's office?"*, which was met not only by a nod to say 'yes', but also with eyes which seemed to imply a kind of sadness at the fact that I was so accustomed to receiving consequences that I knew the process and accepted my fate so easily.

You may have heard that even the seemingly smallest of icebergs can actually be incredibly large. What is seen above the ocean's surface is naught but a glimpse of the true mass of these ship sinking monstrosities. Similarly, I have not been telling you everything, lest the story become repetitive, monotonous, and uninteresting. Suffice it to say, however, that my high school principal was privy to my lengthy record of monstrosities. There was no hiding below any surface for me that day in his office. With simultaneous sternness and exasperation, he told me, *"I see you more often than I see some of my friends, and I would really like to change that"*. In hindsight, I probably should have remained silent instead of suggesting that he get out more. If the actions which had led to this visit had not been the last straw, then my sass most certainly was. Never mind my indignation that the girl-hitter was not receiving equal, if not greater punishment than I. Forget the fact that I had been on the side of justice, doing what was right, protecting the innocent. It was of no value that even Commissioner Gordon was tolerant of Batman's vigilantism. My escalation of misbehaviour was met with an escalation of consequence: I was suspended from school for an indefinite period of time, until I could successfully make a case to the district superintendent as to why I should be allowed to return. I didn't quite understand why I was being handed such a harsh punishment for one punch. After all, it's not like I could have killed him.

I do not recall exactly how long my suspension lasted, but I know it was as short as my mother would allow. As early a time as could be coordinated between her work schedule, because she had to be present, and the schedule of the district superintendent, the appointment was set. In spite of the lockdown my mother imposed during this suspension, she knew that in her absence during her workdays there was no way to enforce any rules which were put into place. She would have no idea how many hours of TV I watched, how many levels I conquered in various video games, or how many kilometers I covered on my bike, and she knew very well that I would do as I pleased when left alone with the opportunity. I do believe that even though she did her part in adding to my punishment, it was half-hearted. She never outright said that she was proud of me for standing up for Jane, but never scolded me either. Believe me, my mother was certainly irate that I had been suspended from school, but it seemed that anger was directed more toward the inconvenience of the whole situation than it was toward me. Her hastening of my return to school was just one more instance of her setting the example that when things go wrong, you make them right. There may be appropriate times for emotional responses, for anger and disagreement, and perhaps even for wallowing. I had to put aside my self-pity about getting caught, my disagreement about whether I had gone too far in the name of justice, and my anger about the entire situation, because none had a place in the superintendent's office when that day did come.

There is something about being sent to the "next level" which can instill a sense of reverence in a person. I must have had that sense of reverence for my high school principal at some point, early on when being sent to his office for one of the first times. There is a centuries-old saying though, *"familiarity breeds contempt"*, which certainly became true after the monotonous repetition of his lectures. Even that last meeting with its escalation of consequence had been rife with the trite admonishments to which I was so accustomed. It should be no surprise then, that as we approached the district office and as we subsequently sat in the outer office awaiting our appointment with the superintendent, I expected more of the same. I knew this time that there was no defending my position regardless of my views on justice, and certainly no room for back-talk. I had left my sassy pants folded in the drawer at home this day. This was a time to sit there, listen, and nod. This was a time to quietly and subserviently agree. Regardless of how familiar the inevitable rambling would undoubtedly be, my limited concept of reverence told me this was a time to pay attention. My concept of reverence would soon grow, and not for the last time in my life.

The moment came when the secretary called on us from her desk, for some reason by name, in the form of a question, even though we had checked in with her upon our arrival and were also the only ones there. This was already much more formal than the *"ok, your turn"* which was sometimes accompanied by an eyeroll which seemed to say, *"him again?"* from the high school secretary.

Should I have worn a tie? It was too late now, and I wouldn't have known how to tie one anyway. Thanks, dad. We were ushered into an office larger than any I had seen in person before, with enough books on every shelved wall to make some small-town libraries envious. The desk was equally grand, yet the man sitting behind it was simply a man, seemingly not unlike many others I had seen. My mother and I sat when he bade us sit, and I awaited the tirade.

I think many of us expect a long, angry eruption to come our way when we know we've done wrong. We try to be good, insofar as whatever "good" means to us. Every non-psychopath has at least some degree of knowledge of right and wrong, whether instilled by parents, society and culture, religion, peer groups, or even a game show host insisting that you phrase your answer in the form of a question. Rest in peace, Alex Trebek. Disobedience and rebellion aside, we don't always do the right thing even when we give our best effort, even if we were so sure of success that we wagered all we had on the Daily Double. When we know we've done wrong, or that we've at least done something contrary to what was expected of our behaviour, we then expect to find ourselves in jeopardy. There is an episode of The Simpsons where Marge competes on the popular game show as a contestant and does so poorly that she finishes in the negative. When the lights go out and the family dejectedly saunters toward the doorway, Alex Trebek's cartoon doppelganger steps in their way, fictional goons at his side, and asks, *"aren't you forgetting something Marge? You were down $5,200. Pay up!"* Many of us go through life keeping score whether we know it or not; not necessarily a score versus any other player, but a score of how much good and bad we've done. A balance sheet of our rights and wrongs, so that when the game is over and the lights go out, we have evidence that we owe nothing; perhaps so that we have evidence we are owed something. Some of us expect that there isn't even a break-even point, some fulcrum upon which our good can outweigh the bad. My teenage self knew that the school office, and now the "next level" district office had a file detailing all of my misdeeds, and so I most certainly believed there was no amount of good in my past which could tip the scales in my favour and earn my way back into school. I expected a long, angry eruption to come my way. Imagine my surprise when I learned from a simple man behind that grand desk in that grand office that I was completely wrong in the way this system worked. In fact, he wanted me to be back in school, because as a child, that was where I belonged.

The tirade never came. Instead, I was asked, "*What will you do when you return to school?*" Interesting; not "if", but "when". I was so taken aback and disarmed by the combination of this unexpected question and the gentle tone with which it was delivered that I temporarily lost contact with the part of my brain where I had stored up all of the arguments I had prepared for this meeting, and so I sat there silent. As if he could read my mind, or at the very least, as if he had experience with these situations, the superintendent broke the silence after a minute or so, "*you're wondering why we're not talking about what you did, aren't you? Well, we both know what you've done, and we both know you've already been dealt the consequences. I want to hear what you will do when you return to school.*" I somehow gathered myself and gave the obvious answer, stating that I would attend all of my classes and stay out of trouble. This was a good starting point, I thought, and the superintendent seemed to agree. He went on though, "*I think you need an outlet. In fact, we all do, so I want to hear within two weeks of your return this Monday that you've signed up for some extra-curricular activity. I don't care what it is. There are a lot to choose from, you will choose one activity to attend either before or after school or during the lunch period, and you will focus your extra energy there instead of channeling it to these behaviours* (gesturing at my file). *If I hear that you do not, or that you do but then begin to miss, you will be back here for a harsher discussion. Understand?*" I said that I understood, and I thanked him while clumsily shaking the hand he had offered. Even in the midst of the grace I had just experienced, a part of me cursed my father because my handshake was neither steady nor firm, which was obviously his fault. Still, the superintendent showed no notice. He seemed satisfied with the whole exchange and was now completing the necessary paperwork with my mother. When that was done, we both thanked him one last time and left, before he could change his mind.

Have you ever tried to open a shaken-up pop bottle? It's possible with some patience. We all know what happens if the cap is simply twisted open and removed. If, by chance, you don't know, then please take the time to go find out. I'll wait here. As a child, I was always told that I should not even try, it would be best to wait, but the truth is you can slowly twist the cap until you hear a slight hiss, and as you see the foam beginning to reach the top, tighten the cap again. If you do this just a few times, you'll have the bottle fully opened in much less time than if you were to simply wait until it was presumably safe to remove the cap in one turn. When I was in high school, I was so shaken up by my past, ready to release my own violent eruption, that there was no way I was ready to believe that God could love me like a father, let alone trust or experience it. I would not have thought at that point in my life that He was concerned not with where I'd been and what I'd done, but with who I'd be and what I'd do. But *"we know that in all things God works for the good of those who love him, who have been called according to his purpose"* (Romans 8:28), and so I think that God was at work in that high school district superintendent's office. I think He was slowly twisting the cap off of my pent up hatred of authority, just until I let out a little hiss, and then replacing it before I could overflow; before I was the one to erupt. God planted a seed that day. He was beginning to show me that he is not interested in score keeping, nor in balance sheets. God had shown me a shadow version of His truth: *"For it is by grace you have been saved, through faith—and this is not from yourselves, it is the gift of God— not by works, so that no one can boast."* (Ephesians 2:8-9). The grace I was given that day was only the tip of the iceberg, the visual representation of a much greater grace which we all receive.

It was much too soon in my journey to make the connection, to see the parallel, but being outside of time God already knew the older, more mature version of me who loves Him. God was putting markers on my roadway which pointed toward Him, calling me according to His purpose, and causing things to work for my good along the way. In fact, God wanted me with Him, because as His child, that is where I belong.

I Tried

"What and how much had I lost by trying to do only what was expected of me instead of what I myself had wished to do?" – Ralph Ellison, Invisible Man

When Starbucks first introduced their instant coffee, they claimed that it was nearly indistinguishable from the real thing. That's right, instant coffee is not real coffee. There was a taste test challenge in one of the stores one day, and when the barista asked me to participate, I simply smelled each of the options and pointed out the imposter. Somewhat indignant at my claim that I could know so easily, she insisted that I actually taste the two samples before coming to a conclusion, so I did. Without hesitation, I stuck with my original choice. When the barista looked for the mark on the bottom of the cup indicating which sample was the instant coffee, she begrudgingly admitted to my success and awarded me with a voucher for a drink on the house. Don't tell me that I can't smell out a fake.

Trying to replace a father's guidance, wisdom, discipline, and love is like trying to replace my coffee with instant, or even decaf. A lot of people can accept the substitution, but that doesn't make it the same thing. Many people who don't experience the craving for the real thing seem to have difficulty understanding those of us with that craving, and our refusal to accept substitutions. We also need to learn and understand for ourselves that no substitution is going to satisfy our craving for a father's love. We need to recognize our craving for what it is, and stop trying to fill it with fakes.

One of the best ways to get me to do something is to tell me that I can't. Thriving on challenge or in a stressful situation has become a useful trait not only in my work life, but in various other scenarios. Analyzing a situation from different angles and proposing potential solutions, regardless of how unrealistic they might sound is a talent which developed over time. One of the actual benefits of growing up without a father to help me overcome certain milestones, or to guide me through smaller situations is that I was forced to figure out a lot of things on my own. Of course, I had some level of help from my older brothers, my mother, and the acquaintances I'd found along the way. Regardless of the dedication and perseverance I did develop through those relationships, there is no substitute for a father to truly and wholly fill that void.

I had tried to find acceptance in friendship. I had tried to break through the stigma of being the baby brother and had hoped to be included in my brothers' lives by choice more than by force. I had tried to be the "good son" for my mother, which had worked to a degree, but through no fault of her own she was not a father. I had tried to be alone, I had tried to bully the bullies, I had tried to fade into the background, and I had tried the mantle of anti-hero. The commonality between all that I had tried, other than the fact that I still felt an emptiness inside, was that I had tried everything without guidance. When my high school district superintendent insisted that as a condition of my return to school from suspension I had to sign up for some extra-curricular activity, that was something which had not previously occurred to me. It was not something which I had tried of my own volition, it was something which an authority figure had guided me toward. Never mind that I was forced into it, a part of me realized at the time that one thing I had not yet tried was listening and obeying, so it was worth a shot. At least, it was worth trying to the extent that I could fly under the radar by checking off the attendance box and appearing to do the right thing.

Of all the available options, the most tantalizing aspiration for me as a teenager was to become some kind of athlete. Those who were a part of a team, and especially those with the prowess to be a catalyst for their team to win were some of the most admired in high school. As much as I may have been deluding myself, making myself believe that I could sustain a façade for the foreseeable future, I was still somewhat realistic in this endeavor. I knew there was no way I would make it on to the football team, the soccer team, the baseball team, or anything else which might have required a father's training from a young age. One thing that I was good at was running. After all, I had plenty of practice running away from bullies who had designated me as an easy target, from older brothers who never seemed to grow out of their desire to practice their wrestling moves, or even from angry drivers with a cracked windshield. The clear choice was to join the track team; not only because I was good at running, but because of the relatively small pool of competitors for a place. There was some competition within the team, but at the time there was only one other boy interested in a place as a long-distance runner, so there was room for us both. Being closely matched in ability, we had no reason to be concerned about the possibility of being cut. There were slots to be filled, and so even if I turned in a poor performance at tryouts, I would still be one of the top two potential candidates. It turned out that all of the training which I had not known at the time was training had paid off; I was not just good at running, I was one of the best.

After successfully becoming a member of the team, I quickly realized another benefit. Not only had I been accepted, but the unique aspect of this team was the lack of dependence upon my teammates which, on the flipside, also meant they would not depend upon and therefore be disappointed by me. We did encourage one another and push one another to be better, but ultimately my success seemed to be completely within my own control. There was no need to worry about whether someone would pass me a ball, there was no physical target at which I had to aim in order to score a goal, and there was no opposing player whose purpose was to interfere with my success. My success was mostly dependent upon my obedience to the coach, my initiative to show up, to train both at practices and on my own time, and my ability to push through any pain that arose. If I could ignore the emotional pain of my abandonment and pretend that everything was fine, it seemed that ignoring a little bit of physical pain should also be possible, and might even be easy by comparison. Remembering how my older brothers would always joke and laugh at the idea of me doing anything athletic just added fuel to the fire which was beginning to grow within me. They may have always disallowed me from participating in any of their activities, but this was finally something of my own. This had become something that only I could tell myself I could or could not do.

Finding this place where I seemed to belong was a joyous experience for me. As children we all have very little, if any control. Those of us who have felt especially helpless as a result of trauma tend to seek out control in our lives. Whether consciously or subconsciously, we desire to determine our own outcomes as we begin to grow older. The less control we have, the greater the desire for it seems to be. Being allowed to control my own success, and even receiving encouragement to do so was something that I came to consciously realize had been missing in my life. Until then, the underlying motives had been auto-pilot behaviours, but now that I had a clear goal to work toward and a place where my only obligation was to do so, I felt that I was in complete control of my own result. Many of us are running toward some goal to prove ourselves worthy, or to prove ourselves better than the assumptions put upon us. Even when we've put those assumptions upon ourselves, the weight of our belief in our alleged worthlessness is a yoke we struggle to throw off. Even if there is no clear goal, the goal may be to run away from something, or simply to run, as if the wind will blow the weight of our past off of our shoulders, for it to never catch up and swallow us.

Ironically, having practically no social life turned out to be a kind of benefit. I never missed a practice, nor did I have competing priorities in the evenings or on weekends, allowing me to train on my own time. I was determined to prove myself. I was finally doing something of my own, and so I was driven to succeed not only by my desire for admiration or acceptance from others, but also to prove to myself that I was capable of independent achievement. After all, if I could succeed on my own, then I could finally say that I didn't need a father; that it didn't matter whether he had ever loved me or wanted to be around me. I wasn't just taking control of my outcome on the track team, I was finally taking control of my feelings and my future. The pain of training, of pushing myself beyond what I thought my boundaries were and breaking them, was worthwhile knowing that the suffering was producing perseverance. This perseverance was, in turn, moulding my character and giving me a hope that I might actually earn the adjective "winner".

The day came when my training would be put to the test. Heading to the city-wide track meet, I knew that my average time for my race length was better than the average for the age range in which I was competing. In fact, it was better by a rather good margin, and I had even beaten the high school record multiple times, though unofficially because it had happened in practice. I therefore knew that if I did all of the right things such as get a good night's rest, hydrate, warm up, and stretch, my win was already a foregone conclusion. In the days leading up to the event, I made sure my water intake was appropriate. I was sure to get enough sleep each night. I continued to stretch, go for a practice run, and stretch again. I did all of the right things, and so I had nothing but confidence as nearly a dozen other boys and I lined up at our starting blocks. When the pistol fired, I flew forward, concentrating only on myself, and not acknowledging the other runners. I knew that in a five kilometer long run my early position relative to the others did not matter. This was a contest of not only speed but also, and possibly more so, of endurance. As I quickly found my pace, the speed to which I had become accustomed in my practices where my average times were above average, I noticed there were no other runners in front of me. A whisper in my mind caused a brief moment of panic that told me I had probably just disqualified myself with a false start, but as they often do, a glance backward revealed the truth. The race was on, and without any more effort than I had been exerting in recent practices, I was in the lead!

Regardless of the course being a predetermined restrictive oval track, the view from the front felt like an affirmation of my sudden freedom. It was a course on which I had chosen to be, and a course on which I was winning. Knowing that looking over my shoulder was wasted energy, and also opened up opportunity for error, I was sure to only sneak half-glances as I rounded the curves where such a vantage point coupled with my peripheral vision would give me some insight, and was encouraged by what I saw each time. Being able to see and count each of the other runners from such an angle meant none were too close behind. As I reached the longer side of the track where each lap would complete, the view in front of me would include the sidelines where I could see the look of pride on the face of my coach. He would even shout the encouragement I had never received from a father as I passed, and, as the race went on, he was not the only one. After a couple of laps, other team members who were either finished or awaiting their turn in their respective competitions were standing at the side of the track, cheering MY name! Some of them were even girls who I would previously have assumed didn't even care to know my name. It was happening. Finally, after taking my own control, after the hard work, the perseverance through the pain, the practice, the discipline, and the realization that I had never needed a father after all, it was happening!

Then, it happened. The stitch in my side like a giant thorn, the agonizing cramp which suddenly reminded me that there must be a God, because in that moment there was nothing I could do about this searing pain other than to beg Him to remove it. Like a person desperate to get their car started in the dead of winter, repeatedly turning the key only to be rewarded with the same frustration, I refused to give up. Though my pace slowed, and my hand adhered itself to my side as if the slight pressure would alleviate the pain, I continued on as best as I was able. Like a ship caught in a sudden storm, my confidence was thrown off course, as if everything I had been running from was my inevitable destination. Something about my posture and possibly even the look on my face as I passed my coach and teammates for the last time, to begin the last lap, must have signaled to them the difficulty I was having. The applause and their shouts of encouragement told me that I could do this, that they each believed I would do this, but the looks on their faces showed the same concern and doubt that was seeping into my heart and threatening to capsize my confidence. Simultaneously wanting to not let them down, and wanting to prove my own doubts wrong, I trudged forward as best as I was able. Even as I was passed by one of my competitors, and then another, and another, until the count of runners in front of me equaled the count that had originally been behind me, I knew my shame would be even greater than it already was if I didn't turn in my best possible time under this cursed circumstance. As I eventually crossed the finish line, I was thankful to be dripping with sweat to the point that it hid my tears. I was devastated to have proven to my peers and to myself that even my absolute best was not good enough.

Homer Simpson once said, "The lesson here is to never try", and in my mind at the time, that was the whisper which I adopted as truth. Trying had been hard work. Trying had taken up a lot of my time. Trying had ignited and elevated my hopes, only for them to ultimately be crushed like a ship's hull against protruding rocks, cast into an abyss where a beast waits to swallow them. Trying had led me to believe that I had some sort of control over my outcome, only to be blindsided by the truth that there are always things outside of our control, in this case the betrayal of my own body. I was too mired in the shame of my loss and my evident worthlessness to my team to realize then that in every area where I did have control, I actually had been successful. That is, up to the point where I had control over my reaction to this loss. I had overcome my initial doubts, my tiredness through practice, and my habits of avoiding others in favour of being on a team. I had ignored the sarcastic barbs of my flock of misfits who probably didn't even realize they wanted me to fail so that they wouldn't feel left behind. I had ignored the physical strain of my training. I had no choice in the matter when during that race a cramp pulled me into those waves of despair.

I did, however, have a choice to continue to train, to stay in shape and even improve for the next year's track season. I could have accepted the comforting words from my coach and teammates for the encouragements they likely were, instead of choosing to believe it was nothing but pity. Yet, assuming the worst possible scenario had become a characteristic of my already broken heart. I chose to believe that all I had accomplished was to shine a light on my worthlessness, while previously the one thing I was at least somewhat good at was hiding. Having no context for how it felt to receive empathy, I ran from what I felt was a torrent of pity. I chose to go back into hiding, to allow myself to be swallowed by the beast of my own shame.

It wasn't until years later that my prideful or even sometimes arrogant "I'll show you!" response to being told I'm incapable of something was redeemed in me to be an asset and a healthy motivational tool. There is a cliché saying, "God doesn't call the qualified, He qualifies the called", but we must realize that often times a saying becomes cliché because it is true. Jesus once said, *"What is impossible with man is possible with God"* (Luke 18:27), it's just unfortunate that at the time, I preferred the familiar comfort of the chains holding me in my dark cave. Trying to step out into the light had felt like standing in a scorching east wind, with the sun beating down on my head, causing me to grow faint, and feeling angry enough to let my hopes die.

He Didn't Have To Be

"What good is the warmth of summer, without the cold of winter to give it sweetness?" – John Steinbeck

"We're getting married!" Even when she scored tickets to see Keith Urban live in concert, I don't think I have ever seen my mother more excited than when she and Mike came home and made this announcement. They had been dating for some time, and he had already moved in, yet this turn of events was still somewhat of a surprise to me. This was a higher level of commitment than I would have expected from the woman who had taught me *"we don't need anyone"*. The other source of confusion came from trying to understand Mike's perspective. As I have tried to convey already, I was not exactly the best kid, not to mention I was only one of three. He was already in the picture well before I was eventually suspended from school that one time, but that doesn't mean I hadn't already provided countless reasons for him to think twice about this commitment. Did he know what he was signing up for? Maybe he did, because the way I saw things, he wasn't signing up for anything more than a wife. Mike already had two daughters of his own. I assumed he wasn't looking to step into any semblance of a fatherly role, not for my brothers and me; especially not me. Nobody would want to. Even when, later that evening, Mike took me aside and told me that he intended to be around for the long haul and that he would never hurt us or leave us, regardless of how much I might have wanted to believe him I still had my doubts. I never voiced those doubts; not to Mike, to my mother, nor to anybody else. Speaking them aloud would not only have been an admission of my insecurity and therefore of my weakness, but would also make what I assumed was his inevitable departure more probable, more real, more true.

Mike turned out to be different from other men my mother had dated. From my interpretation, he had more of a "live and let live" approach with my brothers and me. He certainly never ignored us, nor did he intentionally exclude us, but he also never imposed himself upon us. I'm not sure what he would have done if I had ever outright disrespected him because I never did; at least, not to his face. I had learned my lesson not to do any such thing when a previous potential partner of my mother had responded to my sass with a slap across the face. A very, very hard one. I find it interesting that the man who didn't seem to pull back in the slightest when hitting a child was the same man who would occasionally say *"you know, you can call me dad if you want"*. Mike never once laid his hands on me. He also never tried to force any kind of relationship, let alone a father-son dynamic, other than what developed on its own. Yet somehow, he turned out to be a hundred times the father that other man, and probably many others, could have been. The second biggest regret of my life is that I wasn't aware enough in those years to see the value of what was right in front of me. Instead, like a pearl given to swine, I might as well have trampled this gift underfoot.

Just as my mother did, and like at least one previous boyfriend of hers, Mike worked as a courier driver. I don't know whether there was just something particularly appealing about a professional package-handler. The reality is likely more the fact that a single mother with three boys had very limited spare time, and so the opportunity to grow close to someone was most prevalent at work where she would spend at least forty hours each week. At the time they met and at least for some time after moving in, Mike drove a three tonne flatbed truck. Though it was a company owned vehicle, for the sake of convenience and efficiency after late day deliveries or prior to morning pick-ups he was often allowed to park the truck at home overnight or on weekends. You may never have been a courier driver, but you might have an idea of what happens to your car on a road trip. You pull out from your motel in the morning and head straight to the nearest drive-thru coffee shop. You see those golden arches on the horizon and your stomach demands a pitstop. You begin to accumulate paper cups, paper bags, unused ketchup packets (or were they catsup packets? I still don't know). We all know exactly where all of that trash goes though, on the floor of your vehicle. One of my first paying jobs, before I was old enough to be legally employed, was for twenty dollars every other week to clean out

Mike's truck. Not just pick up the trash, but to vacuum the floor, and to wash all of the windows, dashboard, and inside panels. These days that might sound like a lot of work for twenty bucks, but back then that was a generous payday for a kid my age. Knowing the consequences of being caught stealing cash from my mother's purse, I resolved to do a good job in order to keep this legitimate income flowing.

Somewhere around the time Mike's job circumstances changed such that he would no longer be driving that truck, let alone bringing it home, I had become old enough to deliver newspapers. From what I've heard, it's different these days; there are more restrictions on who can perform this function, not the least of which is a higher age. In fact, at the time I'm writing this I've searched for and found the position posted for a local newspaper, and the ad states applicants "must have a reliable vehicle". I think it's safe to assume that a bicycle does not count. Regardless of how things are today though, I was able to land the job back then at twelve or thirteen years of age, thanks in large part to Mike and the fact that a good friend of his happened to be a manager in the exact area where we lived.

It's interesting that I never asked Mike to speak to his friend on my behalf. I never expressed a desire for his help in getting a job, not even in the earlier circumstance of cleaning his truck. These things were his idea, and not like one of those adult "ideas" which are actually commands for a child to follow. I'm sure that I could have said 'no' just as easily as I had agreed. I'm not sure whether my mother had ever warned him about my earlier transgression, from the pre-Mike era, when money had gone missing from her purse. I have no idea if he had been forewarned to keep a close eye on his wallet, and so I cannot say whether that played into his motivation. He may have been blind to that sin of mine, or he may have chosen to ignore it and focus more on who I could be rather than who I had been. What I do know, now, is that Mike knew how to be a father. He understood that children would have desires, whether for a Slurpee of their own while out on a bike ride with friends, or even for the underlying feeling of inclusion and belonging, the lack of shame at being able to buy their own Slurpee. He understood that people tend to fill their desires one way or another, and so he provided an avenue through which I could do so in a good way, and be instilled with a sense of responsibility along the way.

One summer in my early teens, I wanted a pair of cowboy boots. I had fallen in love with country music, and had recently attended my first ever real life concert where I felt so out of place in my tattered sneakers. There was just something about the leather, the click of the heels on the ground with every step, and the intricate stitching of those boots that lit a covetous spirit within me. To this day, I still can't carry a tune in a bucket, and even then I knew I had no hope of becoming a superstar like the man who tore off the roof of the arena at that concert, Mr. Garth Freaking Brooks. I'm fairly certain that is his actual middle name. I could be a little bit more like him though, even if only in the way I was shod. Fourteen year old me idolized this man. In spite of affording only the cheap seats at the concert, my envy of the people in the front row on the floor overcame me. At one point, I ran to the bottom of the steps, and after a furtive glance in each direction to ensure the security guards were paying attention to something other than me, I hopped the boards and sprinted for the stage. No, I did not jump up there with Garth; I knew better than that, especially seeing that the security guards in position up front were much more attentive than those I had already evaded. Thanks to my scrawny, unathletic frame finally coming in handy for something, I did manage to squeeze my way to the front of the throng of fans where I could reach up in hope of a hand-slap, but alas, Garth was playing guitar. Both of his hands were busy, and it was only a matter of time before my cheap-seat presence was found out and I was evicted. I did the only thing I could. At the opportune moment, I reached out and grabbed Garth Brooks' ankle. It wasn't exactly a vise-like grip, and after a brief glance down and a smile he easily sauntered along to the next fan, but I had had my moment. I strode back to my seat feeling like I had just won the lottery. I bragged for weeks afterward that I had touched Garth Brooks. Okay, fine, for years afterward. I'm apparently still doing it. That is how much I adored this living legend. Yet, I was completely unfamiliar with the concept of budgeting and saving, so my newspaper delivery income was unlikely to earn me those boots. Not to mention, I wanted them NOW.

Jesus once posed the question to a group of people He was teaching, *"Which of you, if your son asks for bread, will give him a stone?"* (Matthew 7:9). A pair of cowboy boots costs more than a loaf of bread, more than even a lot of brand name sneakers, and I was accustomed to knock-offs. Sadidas, if you will. I had already learned through experience that our life circumstances were not such that I could simply ask for and receive everything I wanted from my mother, regardless of how much she might have wanted to give. I literally couldn't ask my father; I knew not which prison he was in, let alone the phone number. Even if I had asked anyone for my "loaf of bread", I'd have expected a stone and been pleasantly surprised to receive that much. There was no way I would have asked Mike, because while consciously I knew he felt no obligation nor desire to provide, subconsciously I believed the inevitable "no" would simply be further evidence toward my lack of worth.

I did what many of us have done, which is something children are especially good at. I dropped numerous, obvious hints. Mike caught on, and though the result was not an immediate gift, it was one of another kind. He soon lined up a few days' work for me at an elderly man's house. At the time, I viewed the man as elderly, though he was likely only in his sixties. I was to scrape and repaint all of the eaves and window frames on this man's house for a pre-negotiated price; one which would bring me very close to my goal. Somehow, this job turned into a lot more, not the least of which was replacing the front walk with new concrete slabs. Those things are still heavy now that I'm fully grown and in much better shape. Back then, I might as well have been building the pyramids by hand. Also back then, I had not yet learned how to stand up for myself. Perhaps more so, I had not yet felt worthy of, well, anything, including a renegotiated wage for expanded job duties.

After another long day of toiling away for this man, followed by the 45 minute bike ride home which was obviously against the wind and uphill, Mike asked why I was grumbling under my breath as I parked my bike in the garage where he was tinkering with his car engine. After some hesitation which came from the fear of saying anything negative about his friend, he eventually got me to admit my dissatisfaction with the expanded job duties. After listening to the whole story, Mike sent me inside, saying nothing other than *"you'd better go wash up, mom will have dinner ready soon"*.

The next morning, feeling as if I had no choice but to follow through on my commitment to finish the work around John's home, and believing it was the only way to be paid at least the amount upon which we had agreed, I dressed and embarked on that 45 minute bike ride to his house, obviously once more against the wind and uphill. When I arrived and began to don my work gloves, John interrupted and called me into the backyard gazebo, where he invited me to sit and start the day with a glass of iced tea. When I obediently sat and began to sip from the glass, I nearly spit the tea right back out when John placed three times the amount of cash he had originally agreed to pay on the table in front of me. As if that weren't enough, imagine my shock at his words, "*here's what I owe you so far, you'll get the OTHER HALF when the work is done*".

"*The Lord hears His people when they call to Him for help. He rescues them from all their troubles*" (Psalm 34:17, NLT). This situation wasn't nearly the same as that of the original audience of those words, but Mike had heard my call for help in spite of my inability to articulate it. I wasn't in a situation where I needed rescue, but Mike had resolved my troubles. Mike never spoke of God, and I am certain that he was not intentionally trying to emulate God, yet he did. Even then, God was trying to show me how good of a father He is through the shadow-version Mike was. Not all shadows are bad; shade can be a wonderful place of rest from the heat. Just as God does for all of us, Mike had stood up for me when I was incapable of standing up for myself. And, when I returned home that day, once again pedalling against the wind and uphill for 45 minutes, I told Mike what had happened, as if he didn't already know. He then said something to me that God is constantly trying to convey to every one of us: "*You're worth it*". Mike has never been a hugger; to this day he resists even when saying goodbye after a once-or-twice per year visit to the town six hours away where he and mom now live, but I suspect he was glad to receive one that day. I know I was more than glad to give one.

God is incredibly generous. Many people believe the opposite to be true, thinking that He imposes unnecessary rules, not the least of which is the concept of a tithe, giving ten percent of your income back to Him through the church. God gave us life, and He sustains it each day. He gave each of us skills and abilities, and placed us into circumstances where those skills and abilities could be used to earn a paycheque. Then, when we receive that money by using the skills and abilities God gave us, He continues to be generous by telling us to keep ninety percent of the take, even though we could have done none of the work without Him. I think a lot of us could be plucked out of our life and placed in a beautiful, paradisiacal garden where we have free reign over every single animal, plant, insect and whatever else is there, with the exception of one fruit tree, and we would still not be happy with the majority percent. We would want that last piece we were forbidden to touch. When it comes to our money, time, and talents we keep repeating the same mistake of the first people, Adam and Eve. We do this not only in our relationship with God, but in our relationships with others as well.

Mike had taught me a few things, such as how to scrape and repaint rain gutters. Through his example and encouragement I learned about the integrity of following through on your commitments; whether to arise early enough each day to deliver newspapers on time or to see a manual labour contract through to the end. Even though there was an unspoken expectation that I was not to impact his reputation by falling short after he had given his personal recommendation for me, he never outright asked for anything in return. It may have been better if he had. Some definition of clear boundaries and a measure of accountability might have prevented me from straying off of the course upon which I had been set; to becoming a more productive, responsible person.

As we grow and gain freedom, oftentimes hearing "you can't" can make us want to do whatever we are being forbidden to do. It's another form of taking control. There are various psychological theories both proven and unproven about how and why people react to that big, shiny red button with the "do not push" sign next to it. Personally, I think there is more to this experiment than what appears on the surface. Based upon what I've already said about this scenario, you might think that I would immediately push the button just because I was told not to, but that is not necessarily a correct conclusion. If my teenage self just happened to come across such a button, then yes, I would have probably pushed it. On the other hand, had I been intentionally put in a room with the button, I would have assumed that the experiment was designed to make me eventually press the button, and therefore would have refused to do so out of simple stubbornness and spite. The difference is in the expectation placed upon me, but the resulting behaviour is the same; refusal to meet your expectation. You're not my father, so you can't tell me what to do.

Adopting that mantra was essentially giving myself permission to do as I pleased. The implication that only my father can tell me what to do, coupled with the fact that I had no father, meant that nobody could intentionally direct, guide, or even influence my attitudes or behaviours. This viewpoint gave me the apparent freedom and control to mould myself in the image of anything of my own choosing. Mike's "live and let live" approach may have made a degree of sense for our situation, but we all need boundaries and accountability lest we end up running amok. Even with a role model such as Mike now in my life, someone who saw worth in me and at least went to the extent to encourage me to grow into a better version of myself, I had already begun to develop a sense of pride.

It may sound strange to hear that I was prideful after everything I've shared about having a lack of self-worth, but pride isn't necessarily a belief that *"I'm so great"*. I certainly did not believe there was anything great about myself. I also did not believe or recognize that I was proud, which is why I allowed myself to become proud. I never saw it coming. 1 Peter 5:8 tells us to *"Watch out for the devil. He prowls around like a lion, looking for someone to devour"* (paraphrase). Interesting that a group of lions is called a "pride". Sidenote: I love lions, they are not the devil, he just wishes he were a lion because they're awesome and he is not. Like a prowling lion, pride snuck up on me and began to devour any humility I might have had. Pride actually coupled itself with my lack of self-esteem in such a manner that I began to simultaneously believe that nobody wanted me, but also that it was OK that nobody wanted me. That I could run this race of life on my own terms, regardless of any outside factors and regardless of my poor track record.

I pointed out earlier that a stereotypical trait of boys is our propensity to get into trouble. This is not something that we usually grow out of before our teenage years, if ever, and I was certainly no exception. Having found some sense of belonging in my high school years with the other outcasts, I began to make choices of my own, to differentiate myself from my brothers and from the image my mother had of who her "baby boy" should be. In retrospect, it's ironic that in my quest to develop my own identity, I was still trying to impress the people around me, and allowing their opinions to influence my decisions. While allowing myself to be fooled into believing I was in control, I would allow my desire to continue these friendships and my need for acceptance to tell me what to do at a subconscious level. While believing that I was consciously not allowing my mother, brothers, stepfather, teachers, or any other authority of this world tell me what to do, I was subconsciously allowing exactly that kind of direction in my life by choosing to always do what was essentially the opposite of their expectation. Without their expectation of my behaviour, I would have had nothing against which to rebel, no opposite course, and therefore no choice between the two.

I may have been the kind of kid to be labelled "geek" or "nerd", and I may have been above average intelligence in a lot of ways, but as you already know that does not mean I made smart choices all of the time. Smart decisions do not lead to imprisonment within one's locker, or to suspension from school. In one way, being more intelligent helped lead me to a path which was not smart at all. One high school teacher had a habit of showing up for class no earlier than the starting bell, and marking his students' absences on the attendance sheet in pencil. This meant I could show up early, erase the previous day's attendance occurrence to show I had been present, then leave before he arrived. I actually was intelligent enough to miss a great deal of this high school physics class and still nearly ace every test. I thought I was equally smart with my devious behaviour, giving myself the control and the freedom to go where I wanted with whomever might accept my presence.

It wasn't long before I and a couple of my misfit acquaintances learned that a lot of the time, sidling up to a smoker who had just lit their cigarette was an opportunity to fit in somewhere. They weren't likely to go anywhere for seven to ten minutes. The problem with this became my lack of ability to participate. Like that one child at the corner store or the ice cream truck unable to buy his own treats, I could only rely on the generosity of others for so long before I would have to pay my own way. Even though cigarettes cost much less then than they do today, there would be limits to others' willingness to give one up, even for the going rate of a quarter. There was also the issue of being too young to legally buy a pack even when I had my own spending money. It was not long before my codependent tendencies began to once again push me across lines of morality.

Mike is a kind and generous man. He is still married to my mother decades after the time of these events. When my wife and I recently took a trip to the town where they now live, he gassed up his boat, he bought bait to take us fishing, he gassed up the ATV so that we could go out exploring, and he shared his beer. On top of not paying for a hotel because we were expected to stay with mom and Mike, they also refused to allow us to spend money on food, neither groceries nor a restaurant bill. In spite of our best efforts to contribute, our contribution was minimal due to their pre-emptive stocking of supplies. Where I would previously take advantage for my own gain, the same source was now openly giving regardless of my attempts at payment. This example of grace and forgiveness from people I took advantage of in my younger years is something I would have benefitted from modeling myself after at that time, but that would have meant allowing an authority figure to have some semblance of control over my identity. I would have had to realize back then that *"you can't tell me what to do, you're not my father!"* was only a convenient excuse, because even if I had a father, I ought to have still respected the other authorities in my life.

As luck would have it back in those teenage years of mine, Mike was a smoker, and had transitioned from driving that three tonne truck around the city to driving an eighteen-wheeler cross-country. He would regularly buy cigarettes by the carton and stash them in the cupboard, then go out on his route, not to return for a few days at a time. Knowing that I was so much smarter than other people, I knew that I could take a pack on occasion without it being missed. I also knew that even if Mike did realize that he knew how to count, it really didn't matter, because he was eventually going to leave us anyway. Regardless of the ways in which Mike had already proven himself, I expected nothing less than abandonment, and so resisted becoming attached enough to feel too guilty about taking advantage of his trust. In spite of what Mike had already given me and done for me, and was in fact continuing to do for me, I wanted more. I wanted what was not being given; what was forbidden. Regardless of the good he had done, which ought to have been more than enough for me, I did not see it as good enough.

In the same way that Adam and Eve were deceived into overstepping their boundaries, I was deceived by my own pride into believing I would never be caught. I may have been quite book smart, but it was foolish of me to think that history would not repeat itself. Noticing the occasional pack of cigarettes missing from a carton is not much different than noticing the occasional bill missing from a wallet. Whether it was the right approach or not, neither Mike nor my mother delivered direct consequences when this particular transgression was found out. Rather, at the dinner table one day Mike just "randomly" commented that since he was buying cigarettes while on the road anyway, it made sense not to leave any behind when he would go to work. He may have even been looking directly at me while speaking those words, but with my downcast eyes I did not notice. What I did notice for a period thereafter was an ebb in the warmth that had previously been growing between us.

One of the most fatherly acts from Mike that I can remember came one day a couple of years prior to my theft of his cigarettes. When a particular repeat bully harassed me on the way home from school yet again, claiming that if he saw me on "his street" one more time he would beat me to the point that I would be hospitalized, I ran home and retrieved a baseball bat. I may not have been capable of connecting that bat with a ball that was hurtling toward me, but I had confidence in my ability with a much larger target. Just as I was headed back out the door, Mike was headed in. It did not occur to me until a much later time that he was home unusually early that day, as if by some divine intervention. The bat in my hands must have seemed unusual to him, especially when coupled with the tears on my face. He simply took the bat out of my hands and said, "I'm not letting you do this."

This man who knew in an instant what I had been planning that day, and knew the consequences would send my life on a downward spiral further than I was already headed, is the man who I assumed would not be smart enough to miss a pack of cigarettes now and then. This man who, on the night he successfully proposed to my mother, came to talk to me and promise that he would never leave or do anything to hurt us is the man who I believed at my core was no different and would eventually abandon us. This man who gave me an opportunity at a relationship with a male role model, who gave me the chance to earn some spending cash on occasion by cleaning his truck, who gave me his trust, was repaid his good with evil. Sometimes that's the problem with deciding everything for yourself. Having freedom to choose what has been forbidden allows us to choose poorly. Without the humility to seek, find, and accept proper guidance, I followed my pride in myself and the belief that I could not count on anyone else. I projected the only image of a father I had ever known onto Mike, and therefore could not see past that projection and appreciate what was truly there. I chose to perpetuate behaviours which I ought to have already learned would lead to consequence. Somehow, the potential for acceptance from random smokers who should have been obvious poor choices as friends outweighed the potential consequence of being caught stealing again. Even when a part of that consequence was the broken trust and loss of respect from people who already loved and accepted me, I chose to betray them. I chose to steal, to kill off that trust and to destroy that respect.

I can tell you from experience that, as it is written, pride does indeed lead to a fall. Most of the time when we fall, it's either by accident, or possibly the result of being pushed. We generally do not see it coming. I hadn't consciously realized that with each lie I told, I was becoming more prideful about my ability to get away with lying. Becoming increasingly adept at convincing others of my untruths was the stumbling block for which I was headed. From pretending that nothing was wrong on the inside, to dodging and deflecting blame, to building a false persona, to convincing others I had something to give, each successful deceit was another brick in my castle which eventually turned out to be a prison of my own making. I also became quite adept at convincing myself that I was doing just fine without a father. The problem was that I didn't know then what I know now. Jesus says, *"If God were your Father, you would love me, because I have come to you from God...you are the children of your father the devil, and you love to do the evil things he does. He was a murderer from the beginning. He has always hated the truth, because there is no truth in him. When he lies, it is consistent with his character; for he is a liar and the father of lies"* (John 8:42-44, NLT). It turns out, I had a father all along, and I was following his example.

Something To Be Proud Of

"The fault, dear Brutus, is not in our stars, but in ourselves." – William Shakespeare, Julius Caesar

With indignation, the words *"What, are you stupid?"* were practically spit in my face. I felt my cheeks flush as I was overcome with embarrassment at this question from Randall, the manager of the retail store where I had my first real, adult job. At sixteen years old I already knew that I was far from stupid, getting straight A's in my classes in spite of skipping many of them and rarely studying for tests. The implication that by some new standard against which I had never before been measured, that by comparison to people out in the real world I was now below average intelligence, immediately shattered my confidence. The one area where I had been able to take pride in myself was suddenly assaulted by the same feelings of inadequacy which had permeated other aspects of my being. Here I was, being publicly berated for my error, and what had I done to deserve this?

Shopping malls seem to hold some kind of magnetism for teenagers, and the one located in between my high school and our home was no different, nor was I. At least, not in that regard. It was also convenient that I was at the mercy of the timetables followed by public transit, and needed to transfer from one bus to another every day right out front of this mall. I would often take advantage of the freedom this layover provided to kill some time inside, especially on the rare occasions when I had some cash burning a hole in my pocket. There was always more merchandise than cash though, and so when I heard the sounds of construction coming from behind a boarded up storefront, I approached to read the "help wanted" sign posted next to the "keep out" and "hard hats required" notices. I'm still not sure why I would need a hard hat to keep out of the construction area, but those were the instructions nonetheless. Regardless, focussing on the other sign, I was smart enough to glean that a new menswear store would be opening and would require all levels of staff. Smartphones didn't yet exist outside of science fiction, so I pulled a pen and paper out of my backpack and wrote down the mailing address and the requirements. I had never written a cover letter in my life and had not yet developed a resume, but I was certain that I was smart enough to produce one of each. I did exactly that the same evening after whipping through my homework, and then stayed late at school the next day in order to transcribe both from notebook paper to nicely typed versions on one of the computers in the library. This was not so long ago that computers and printers weren't already common household items, but my mother chose to spend her hard earned money on more frivolous things such as food and clothing.

A few short weeks later on one of my trips to the mall, I saw that the plywood boards had come down and the store had opened. In spite of my immediate sense of failure and my lack of a hardhat, my curiosity overcame the voice in my mind saying *"see? You aren't good enough for this either!"* and I nonchalantly wandered inside. It wasn't long before I was greeted with the usual *"can I help you find anything?"* which is free to any visitor, and so with nothing to lose I asked whether they were still hiring, and was directed to the back of the store where I met Edward, the assistant manager. Perhaps I was running on adrenaline at that point, because somehow I got through the conversation which, as it turned out, had become an impromptu interview. I walked away with a position as a sales associate, starting the following week.

When I gave my mother the news and she initiated the obligatory discussion about how unacceptable it would be if my grades were impacted, I managed to convince her I could handle both work and school. Furthermore, I managed to negotiate a loan from her so that I could purchase enough dress clothes to get me through to my first paycheque. After all, I couldn't sell suits while wearing jeans. After accomplishing this feat, I sure didn't feel stupid. Then, my first day of work arrived.

Edward had handled the interview, paperwork, and scheduling, so I had not even met Randall until I arrived for my first shift. After a brief introduction, it was straight to work, and I was determined to earn the respect and pride of this male authority figure. I soon learned that his concept of "training" was to tell me what to do, when to do it, and how I had done it wrong. The first task he gave me was to help him put sale tags on some items at the front of the store which were being reduced in price, and so he sent me to the rear where the cashier's desk was located with the instruction to retrieve the sale tags from a drawer beneath. I easily read the labels on each drawer and located the proper one, reached inside, and grabbed the first stack of tags I came across. Perhaps I had been too eager to please, omitting the step of actually reading the tags, because when I returned to the front of the store and held them out to Randall, that is when I heard those words. *"What, are you stupid? These are the '2 for 1' tags, who told you to get these? Take them back, and do it right this time."*

As I trudged back through the entire store and approached the desk again, there must have been a telling look on my face, because Melissa, the cashier, said *"don't take it personally. That's just how he is. Here, these are the tags he wants."* I thanked her as we exchanged the wrong tags for the right, yet even as we also exchanged smiles I was wondering, if she had heard Randall from this distance, how many others had? Determined to at least get through this one day, I put on my best poker face, turned around, and strode back toward both the front of the store and Randall's glare. After sheepishly handing over the correct tags and quietly listening to his further instructions, the rest of that day held nothing especially eventful. I shadowed the boss man and learned a few things, like how to look up pricing of items missing tags, when to replenish inventory and where in the stockroom to locate the appropriate items, to always drop everything else in favour of an opportunity to sell something, and various other normal retail store duties. One particular lesson I learned from Randall not only that day, but throughout my tenure as his employee was one which I deemed most important of all though. It was to walk on eggshells around the man in authority. I learned to assume that I had to always do the right thing the first time in order to please him, and that anything less would be met with guilt and shame. If I had done anything stupid that day, it was to take that lesson too seriously.

Up until that time, any authority in my life had been either circumstantial or imposed. I hadn't chosen my mother and stepfather, nor my teachers. Police and government are simply a fact of life. Even in my previous jobs, in spite of agreeing to take them on, I had been somewhat corralled into subservience. For the first time, I had chosen to place myself under the authority of another, and it had become apparent that I would have to weigh the benefit of the paycheque against the risk of Randall's ridicule and my resultant resentment. We often face this kind of decision in life. Governments and organizations sometimes pay ludicrous sums of money for a third party to complete a "cost – benefit analysis" in order to help them navigate the process, as if the additional cost of the report somehow mitigates the risk of the original cost. Without the means to source outside assistance, I unilaterally decided upon toughing it out. The benefit of making my own money and the relative freedom provided by a steady income far outweighed anything Randall could throw my way. I had already spent years being made fun of, being picked on, and feeling unworthy. At least in this context, I was developing new skills as a side effect. Also, as rough and gruff as he could be, Randall was far from being an ogre. His skin wasn't even green. Over time, as my performance improved both as an employee and in my ability to read his moods, we began to get along quite well. He even seemed pleased, and dare I even say impressed by my sales numbers once I found my pace. It seemed as though all that practice I had lying was coming in handy; I became a rather good salesperson. The benefits of this arrangement were compounding while the risks were ebbing.

When we face a decision whether to humble ourselves before another without expectation of an immediate benefit, then it is more difficult to do so. I certainly balked at the idea when it was first presented to me. The confidence I had gained through my work was beginning to show up in other areas of life. Being forced to approach strangers and open a conversation as they entered my store, and developing indifference to the majority response that I could go fly a kite helped me to take more chances socially, even with girls. Beth and I had met through mutual acquaintances, and would have considered one another friends in spite of our relationship having been confined to school. It seemed like an easy first step to suggest that we hang out at the mall after one of my shifts, because even if "hanging out" might have seemed like a date, I didn't use the d-word. If I were shot down, I could have claimed that I had no such intention, but surprisingly she agreed.

Over time we became more familiar with one another and the relationship progressed. We would spend more and more time together, but never on a Sunday. The way Beth was raised, Sunday was a family day, always beginning with church in the morning. She had never seemed to be a religious or spiritual person, yet she insisted that if things became more serious between us, my attendance at church on Sundays would become an expectation. The additional comments about how her family would be the ones sitting in the very back making sarcastic observations might have been a tactic to make the proposition seem more appealing to me, but only achieved the opposite. If that was one of the few benefits of attending the church service, then what was the point? I could already be a smartass anywhere, anytime. I didn't need to wake up early every Sunday and endure what I viewed as a load of rhetoric about the God who had refused to answer me in my time of trauma.

I saw no benefit whatsoever to putting myself under the authority of Beth's family values, or of a priest, pastor, or minister. I certainly didn't see any benefit to even considering humbling myself before God. People could tell me that God is great, and God is good, but I was more inclined to believe it was all smoke and mirrors, a show being put on by a man behind a curtain who was not "Great and Powerful" at all. A fraud, a humbug, the kind of man who would take advantage of a child who just wants to go home, and make empty promises to accomplish his own goals. Where had God been when I made it through all of those tearful nights as a young child? Where was He when I was either being beaten up or completely ignored by my own brothers? What did He ever do to help keep me out of trouble in school? I had learned to be tough on my own. I had overcome so many obstacles in the absence of both God and a father. I was doing just fine on my own, so what could God possibly provide? From what I knew of God, we had to walk on eggshells around Him, and always do the right thing the first time in order to please Him, because anything else would be met with heaps of guilt and shame. That is, if He could be bothered to show up at all, which I doubted.

Living under our own power, relying only on ourselves may seem like the smart decision, especially if we have a good track record. It's definitely the more tempting route to take if we view the alternative as autocratic or dictatorial. Even those of us who have had success as a result of gentler guidance are prone to take matters into our own hands, perhaps in a moment of impatience or fear. There was once a man named Saul who learned the hard way that doing so often leads to heartache and pain. He lived in Israel long before Jesus bridged the gap between us and God, during the time when God would have a single representative seer or prophet guiding His people. When Saul was about to meet the prophet Samuel for the first time, he was told by some ladies from whom he asked directions, *"As soon as you enter the town, you will find him before he goes up to the high place to eat. The people will not begin eating until he comes because he must bless the sacrifice"* (1 Samuel 9:13). Yes, a man asked women for directions! One of the very first things Saul learned about God's representative was that waiting for him would result in blessing. He was originally looking for some lost donkeys, and had hoped this seer could point him in the right direction, but as it turns out God had an even better plan for Saul. The short version is that Samuel told him he would become the leader of all Israel, and oh, by the way, somebody else has already found the donkeys, so don't worry about them anymore. Instead, *"go down ahead of me to Gilgal. I will surely come down to you to sacrifice burnt offerings...but you must wait seven days until I come to you and tell you what to do."* (1 Samuel 10:8) For the second time, Saul heard that good things come to those who wait; especially those who wait for God's plan to unfold in His timing. Sure enough, the result was that when Samuel showed up, he called the people of Israel together to fulfill their request that he set a king over the nation, and Saul was the one chosen.

Initially, there were some jealous haters who refused to acknowledge Saul as king, but that is to be expected when good things happen to us. We can learn from Saul's reaction, or lack thereof. He simply went about his business, until one day word came from a corner of the nation that a rival king was threatening to invade. Saul mustered up an army and defeated the attackers, after which he was celebrated for his leadership. The people even wanted to thank him by finding and punishing those naysayers, but Saul decreed they be forgiven. Here we have a man who would spend three days wandering around trying to track down lost donkeys. A man who would be humble enough to ask women for directions – no small feat! A man who forgave people who called him unworthy. A man who had repeatedly seen and reaped the rewards of patiently waiting for God's plan to unfold. So, when Saul later led his army against one much larger than his own, we should assume that he once again must have adhered to Samuel's instructions and waited patiently for God's blessing before acting. Yet, seeing how fear was overcoming his troops, Saul grew impatient while waiting and decided to do Samuel's job, offering sacrifices to God. He thought he was doing the right thing, and it might sound that way to us as well. What is wrong about seeking God's blessing? Yet, when Samuel arrived shortly thereafter and Saul apprised him of the situation, Samuel replied *"You have done a foolish thing. You have not kept the command the Lord your God gave you; if you had, he would have established your kingdom over Israel for all time"* (1 Samuel 13:13).

The issue was trust. God had already told Saul to once again wait for Samuel to arrive and offer the sacrifice, then Saul's army would win. Saul did not trust God in the face of fear, and seemed to believe that he could take matters into his own hands, and grasp victory by his own power. He thought he could force blessing out of God sooner than the time God had already planned to bless him. I'm sure at some point in my childhood, I was promised dessert, and then whined and threw a fit demanding I get it NOW, resulting in my mother telling me that behaving in such a way would mean I get none after all. When I was six years old, I would have thought that meant she was mean. When we are older and wiser, we ought to have learned that impatience and a lack of trust can have consequences. The consequence for Saul was that someone else would become king.

We now live in a time when Jesus has bridged the gap between us and God. We do not need a particular seer or prophet to access His guidance, we just need to listen, trust, and be patient. We need to be aware that the authority figures and father figures in our lives cannot measure up to His perfect love, and that many will not even try. The lessons learned from managers, teachers, sometimes even preachers, and especially fathers can wound us, but projecting their failures onto our father God and refusing to trust Him is going to result in consequences only for ourselves. When God puts signposts on our path encouraging us to get to know Him better, perhaps through the example set in a relationship with someone or even as an ultimatum for that relationship to continue, we're the ones who lose out on blessing when we turn the other way.

Mistakenly believing that God cared more about what I did than about me, that He would insist I get everything right the first time "or else", I looked directly at an obvious, blatant signpost pointing toward a potential relationship with Him and said "nope". I turned the other way, and in addition to losing a relationship in the process, I'm sure I also missed out on blessings which were waiting on the path of humility and patience while I continued to take wrong turns.

Looking back at the version of me who was repulsed by the idea of pursuing God, all I can say to my younger self is, "*What, are you stupid?*" My father made a choice without anyone forcing his finger to the trigger, not even God. He was allowed to make that choice, just as God allowed me to make my own choices, and we each experienced the consequences. Yet, there was always a new day regardless of how tear-filled the night had been. When I was much too young to walk home from school on my own, I somehow made it, as if under some protection. God gave me a mother who did everything she could to raise me right and never deserved to be compared to some arbitrary measurement of "enough". God gave me older brothers who, in spite of their normal treatment of me, would occasionally say "*I love you*" in their own way, such as telling a bully "*nobody beats up my little brother except me!*" God introduced to me a kind and graceful school superintendent. God gave me an incredible stepfather. God intervened in many situations throughout my life, through many people. Even when I ignored, avoided, and even insulted Him, God took care of me. I refused to see it, or to even be willing to see it, so if that made me stupid, then the answer was "yes", and I stayed that way for a while longer.

A Place In The Sun

"Most people are far too much occupied with themselves to be malicious." –
Friedrich Nietzsche

Would you voluntarily stand in the way of something travelling 299,792,458 meters per second? What if you didn't have a choice? You actually wouldn't have time to even realize you were in the path of something rushing forward at such a speed, let alone react. The outcome of this scenario seems inevitable regardless of the shape and size of the object hurtling toward you. On average, a bullet leaves a rifle's barrel at 1,200 meters per second, so imagine the result of standing in the path of a projectile moving nearly 250,000 times as fast as a bullet. If you're imagining your destruction, you're correct. The good news is that the only thing we know of that travels 299,792,458 meters per second is not any kind of physical projectile, but light. The light of the sun travels 93 million miles through space to reach Earth, and at the end of its journey, you stop it without even trying. You unwittingly cast a shadow simply by existing. We are told *"God is light; in Him there is no darkness at all"*. (1 John 1:5) I would imagine that the light of God is even greater than the light of the sun He created. Would you voluntarily stand in the way of this light? Are you blocking it without even trying, without even realizing? Even if it isn't always done consciously, it's possible that you and I are casting more shadows than we realize.

In A. A. Milne's popular Winnie the Pooh literature, the character Eeyore is well known for his despondent attitude. Given the opportunity, he seems to point out that every silver lining has a cloud. Even when he wishes someone a good morning, he adds on "if it is a good morning, which I doubt". If you didn't read that quote in Eeyore's voice, I'm disappointed in you. I used to work with a woman who reminded me very much of Eeyore, because in each and every conversation with her she seemed to be dealing with some black cloud which was following her around, raining only on her. Personally, I try to stay away from absolute statements such as "you always", or "you never", but in this case, there is no exaggeration. She was the kind of person who could find a hundred dollar bill on the ground and bemoan the likelihood that it is covered in millions of microscopic germs. She is a more extreme example of a person whose auto-pilot attitude casts shadows of despair upon those around her, but in the same way that we can prevent small fender-benders by imagining the worst case crash that drunk or distracted driving can cause, this extreme case of shadow casting can actually lead us to enlightenment. Recognizing that I did not want to spend time listening to the constant pessimism should, if I am in a healthy mental state, act as a catalyst to encourage me to examine whether there are times when I cast a similar shadow. We sometimes say "*at least I'm not that bad*" when we encounter negative traits or behaviours, but that statement allows us to stagnate. Asking ourselves "*am I like that, even slightly?*" moves our thoughts from judgment to a growth journey.

It is easier said than done, to realize and admit that some piece of us is broken. Hiding in the darkness of denial is especially easier when we find a community of like-minded individuals. We feel better about ourselves when we're not around people who seem better than us, and even more so when we're around people about whom we can say, "*at least I'm not as bad as them*". The apparent solace we find in being accepted by other captives of the same illusions as our own is another shadow version of acceptance. Being accepted for reflecting other people's shortcomings is still not acceptance of you. It's another attempt at trying to fit a square peg into a round hole; you might be able to force yourself to fit in by cutting corners, but you do not belong there if you have to become a different person to be accepted. Stepping out of the shadows can be difficult and frightening, like stepping out of Plato's cave.

When illuminated by the light, we can be truly seen not only by others but also by ourselves. Realize, though, that God already sees you, through and through, and regardless of what you might believe He sees, He sees His child. He sees the best version of you, someone you are capable of becoming. Getting there may mean admitting brokenness and seeking restoration. That sometimes means our social circles need to change; either the people around us need to also work towards becoming healthier people, or we need new social circles. If we confront someone on their perpetual pessimism, or any other negative behaviour, we risk the possibility that we appear hypocritical. We also risk the possibility of being rejected. Our rejection might not even require an outright, overt challenge. Another person can feel confronted about their behaviours simply by our stance that we do not wish to mirror or perpetuate the same behaviours ourselves. Rather than view our social circle as a team where we encourage one another, and push one another to be better, we sometimes tend to find places where our broken selves can remain broken. We go on as fragmented individuals who might happen to exist within a pack so that we may experience the alleged strength and safety in numbers this existence provides.

Wolves hunt as a pack because it generally takes a number of wolves to bring down their prey. The ability to cut an animal off from its herd, to surround it, to distract it from the gnashing teeth on its opposite side makes the hunt a much easier endeavor than for a lone wolf. In spite of this being a team effort, wolves don't generally seem to encourage one another to become stronger. An alpha wolf wants to remain the alpha wolf. A wolf who knows he is not the alpha, and has no chance of beating the alpha in a fight does not always leave the pack for greener pastures. He often stays where there is relative strength, and safety, and comfort. Where there is relatively less risk of failure. A wolf, however, has a very different definition of failure than a sheep does. We humans often fail to realize that our definition of failure, much more like that of the wolf, can drive us to behaviours akin to blocking out the light and stalking through the darkness.

I remember the Friday immediately after my Big Brother turned eighteen years old, and was therefore able to legally consume alcohol. He was allowed to accompany mom and Mike to a bar they would sometimes go to with some co-workers, one of whom seemed to think it would be fun to test Big Brother's constitution. As the youngest, I obviously wasn't there, but in my imagination I can see Big Brother doing his absolute best to match this grown man drink for drink, stubbornly refusing to admit that he had nowhere near the same tolerance, if he even realized this fact for himself. I can hear Mike saying *"let him have his fun, he'll learn his lesson"* in response to mom trying to intervene with silly things like common sense and wisdom. I can even picture this co-worker going behind mom's back and continuing to order drinks for

Big Brother in spite of her objections, because I've not only known people who perform this rite of initiation, to my dismay I must admit that I've done it myself.

I was there to witness the end result. I was able, barely, to make out the words *"I'll never drink again"* from Big Brother's mouth as Mike literally carried him through our living room and upstairs to his bedroom. I don't use the word "literally" as liberally as some people; Big Brother's feet did not touch the floor. I was there to witness the inevitable hangover the following morning, or, perhaps it was afternoon before I saw Big Brother again. I was also there on subsequent weekends which soon proved the adage, *"you should never say never"*. I cannot presume to know the co-worker whom I had been told was the instigator of intoxication on that first outing, and so I have no right nor reason to blame him for any pattern which might have resulted from Big Brother's later choices. He may not have known the shadow he was casting. He may have been completely unaware of his own blind spots, and equally unaware of any possible tendency to prove himself the alpha of that pack by drinking some pup under the table. He may have had no insight to the possibility that he was instilling a sense of failure in Big Brother by alleging that success was defined by one's alcohol tolerance. He most certainly couldn't have known the ripple effect which caused waves in my own life a few short years later.

The false freedom of fatherlessness in which I had chosen to believe led me to follow in the footsteps of any alpha which was heading in an appealing direction. History soon repeat itself when my eighteenth birthday arrived, and Big Brother had the benevolence to bring me out to the favourite watering hole of the pack to which he belonged. As was the case with mom and Mike's co-worker, Big Brother and his friends likely did not know the shadow they were casting. They certainly would not have known of the insecurities within me which were being triggered by this unspoken competition in alleged manliness. If there had ever been some possibility of empathy in that regard from Big Brother, it seemed as though he had drowned it long prior. My past had taught me that as the new guy, I had to prove myself. If I didn't show that I was capable of being a part of the pack, that I was "good enough", I would be left behind yet again. What I viewed as a rite of passage, with each shot representing another milestone to complete in this test of endurance, they may have simply viewed as a birthday celebration. If any of these young men were encouraging me beyond my capabilities or my own well-being, it was likely not a conscious decision to do so. It was, however, a conscious decision on my part, a predetermined goal going into that night, that I would prove I could drink just as much as the next guy. It turns out that I had actually been correct about that part; I just couldn't keep it down as well. Rather than realize my failure to accept shepherding toward better decisions from better influences, I chose to define failure as my inability to keep up with the pack. The problem then, was that in order to consider myself successful, I would have to become better at becoming worse.

I cannot specifically recall whether I uttered the same phrase Big Brother had at the end of his eighteenth birthday, *"I'll never drink again"*, but it is safe to say that I cannot recall the majority of that evening's specifics. Regardless of any promise I may or may not have made to myself or anyone else who may have been listening, it's unfortunate that my mind and heart did not reject the poisonous thoughts and feelings which were pulling me like an undertow as easily as my stomach rejected the alcohol. It seems that I had developed a much higher tolerance for being disappointed in myself, for experiencing the shame of not successfully integrating to the pack, for viewing myself as the weak link and assuming that others saw me in the same way. Unlike with the high school track team, these poisonous thoughts were not a deterrent which discouraged me from trying harder, striving for success. Also unlike the track team, there was no coach nor teammates encouraging me to find success, and modeling a definition of success which would be healthy. Left once again to my own devices, the standard by which I measured myself became one which was destructive. I accepted the disappointment of knowing I would never be the alpha of this pack, and the shame of being invited only as Big Brother's tag-along. The relative safety of inclusion I was afforded in return for being the one to whom others could point when they said *"at least I'm not as bad as that guy"* was, in my warped opinion, better than the seclusion of abandonment.

Even as I began to develop my own circle of friends and distance myself from Big Brother's pack in favour of one where I seemed to have greater status, I surrounded myself with people who would encourage me to perpetuate the same behaviours which were already becoming not only a habit, but a lifestyle. By this time, Randall had moved on from that menswear store where I worked, Edward had taken on the manager role, and I had earned the assistant manager position. Edward and I had become good friends, and even though he was a few years older and not the "hang out in a club every weekend" type, alcohol was just a part of socialising. It's likely that his age, even a couple of years greater than that of Big Brother, coupled with not only his acceptance of me but his actual desire to be my friend made it that much easier for me to consider Edward a role model. He seemed to have his life pretty much in order, with a house of his own, a car, and a steady relationship. When we would go out for dinner and it was accompanied by highballs, that just seemed natural. When a meal wasn't even involved and we would end a day of work by heading to the lounge of the restaurant attached to the mall solely for a couple of drinks, that became normal. In addition, because back then you could smoke pretty much anywhere, it seemed like I should pick that habit back up as well since Edward shouldn't have to smoke alone. I was making my own money, and was now old enough to buy cigarettes instead of risking the consequences of stealing them from someone else. Again, by my own decision, my own desire to fit in, I succumbed to the darkness of the shadow cast upon me.

We're called to step out of the shadows. We're told *"Do not conform to the pattern of this world, but be transformed by the renewing of your mind. Then you will be able to test and approve what God's will is – His good, pleasing and perfect will."* (Romans 12:2) Even though we're also told in Romans 1:20 *"God's invisible qualities—his eternal power and divine nature—have been clearly seen, being understood from what has been made, so that people are without excuse."*, my focus was on things which I had been taught to consider good and pleasing. The examples all around me were far from divine in nature. Even my hero Garth Brooks sang about having friends in low places, *"where the whiskey drowns and the beer chases our blues away"*. Yet, in spite of every negative influence and temptation, the infallible word of God says that I had *"no excuse for not knowing Him"*, regardless of how many I may have tried to make. I would like to claim ignorance, because at that point in my life nobody had told me about God, but hadn't I inferred His existence already, crying out to Him as a child? Had the absence of receiving the exact answer for which I had hoped back then caused me to believe He must not exist? Even if that were so, His very creation by which I was surrounded was calling me to question... what, exactly? Where it all came from? Where I came from? Why I am?

The evidence of God's goodness was, and still is and always will be, all around me. Unfortunately, I tuned out the still, small voice, as we are all prone to do when we set up some idol before Him, some totem which grows taller and taller the more we revere it, the more we give it power. The larger it becomes, the more light it blocks and shadow it casts, not only perpetuating but increasing its influence. We believe that we have the freedom to roam within our desires, but it is only freedom to roam within the shadow cast by that desire, and the prospect of moving out into the light becomes more and more frightening as we acclimate ourselves to our self-imposed boundaries. We believe the lie that God wants to impose rules to restrict us, but in reality when we have no idol before Him and instead obey Him, the shadows dissipate, there is nothing left but light, and we are truly free to roam. With all due respect to Garth Brooks, I think he got it wrong, and he was only one letter off. There is evidence of God all around us, but *"the whiskey drowns and the beer chases our clues away"*.

The concept of darkness is just that, a concept, or a perception. Light is scientifically defined as a form of radiation, or energy. Light exists, and the concept of darkness is simply a descriptive term to explain the absence of light. Remember that *"God is light, and there is no darkness in Him at all"* (1 John 1:5), and so in His presence there are no shadows. Outside of His presence, we all cast shadows. Only by becoming completely transparent can we cast no shadow, both literally and figuratively. I'm rather certain that neither you nor I will ever achieve literal, physical transparency. In the metaphorical sense, we might also never fully achieve it until God calls us home. In the meantime, we're free to block out the light. We're free to fool ourselves into believing the lies of our idols. We're free to follow any alpha allowing us to fit in with their pack. Conversely, we're free to find actual belonging with our Creator, our Father, our God as a part of His family. If only I had chosen the latter at that stage in my life, I would have been saved from a lot of heartache.

That Ain't No Way To Go

"Like a thief in the night, you ran away with my heart." – Brooks & Dunn

I had barely made it through the front door and hadn't even removed my coat before she ran up and wrapped her arms around me. For what seemed like the first time in my life, somebody was not just glad for my presence, but actually eager to see me, and I was equally as eager to see her. Whatever feelings I may have had about any other human being up to this point paled in comparison, and we had only known one another for a month or two. Feelings are certainly heightened when they are new, at the onset of a relationship, but this was more than that. This was something I had not sought out, perhaps because I had never known it was something I wanted. Now that LeAnn was in my life her happiness and well being had become a driving force, a major contributor to my purpose. I felt that I would do anything to perpetuate this reciprocal, unconditional love and to protect her. Ironically, I thought I would kill for her. Some dormant piece of my heart had awakened to enable me the capacity to love not only my then-girlfriend Marianne, but this year-and-a-half old daughter of hers as well.

It started on a weekend like many others from that era; at the local bar where even the weak links of the pack were encouraged to display whatever plumage they might have in an effort to attract the opposite sex. Yes, I know that wolves don't have plumage. Not all metaphors have to be perfect in order to make a point. Some time into the night, this young woman caught my eye, and we seemed to be exchanging glances across the room, but my low self-esteem kept me from complete certainty that she was indeed looking at me rather than past me. As it does though, the liquid courage eventually overrode my thoughts, and I found the nerve to begin moving in Marianne's direction.

I looked up once again, and didn't make it a single step because she had disappeared. Kicking myself, my heart sinking, I pulled a cigarette from my pack, lit it, and just as I was flipping my Zippo closed I heard from behind me, "can I get a light?" I turned to oblige and nearly dropped my lighter when I saw that it was her. This icebreaker was a confirmation that she had been looking not past, but at me, and her decision to make the first move implied a mutual interest. I don't recall the specifics of the conversation which ensued, but it must have gone well because the next morning when I reached for that first cigarette of the day, I found her name and phone number scrawled on the flap of the pack.

As these stories tend to unfold, our first phone call led to our first date, which led to our first kiss, and yadda yadda yadda, we were a couple. If you're wondering the same thing George Costanza wondered when his girlfriend used that phrase, you can keep on wondering. If you're wondering who George Costanza is, I'm sorry for your lack of exposure to fine culture. Marianne and I were together just long enough and had gone just deep enough for me to be hooked when she broke the news, "*I have a daughter*", but not so long into our relationship that I couldn't understand her reasons for not telling me sooner. Of course I was intimidated by the idea at first. I was not yet old enough to have ever considered whether this was something I wanted. I had a steady job, but if things progressed far enough this responsibility would mean redirecting at least some part of my income. The manner in which I spent my time would have to change as well; sure, Marianne had been able to make her way out to the bar the night we met, and out for subsequent dates, but those and similar things would certainly not be the priority. Perhaps the most daunting aspect, though, was what the relational dynamic would be like with the father. Marianne assured me that he was not in the picture, nor had any interest whatsoever in being a part of their lives, but it would always be in the back of my mind. If I were to step into this role, I would be a usurper, a pretender who could be dethroned at any moment by the one whose place I had taken. As far as I had come in building up some semblance of self respect and confidence, there was still a little boy inside of me who knew he could be tossed aside and abandoned if the circumstance to do so arose.

Regardless of the fear and insecurity, a greater force was pulling at me. A part of it might have been the desire to stay coupled with Marianne, knowing that to do so I would have to fulfill a role in LeAnn's life, but if that is the case it was a very small, short-lived factor. My desire to defy expectations could have played a role, knowing that most would turn and run; I wanted to be able to say I'm better than that. Amid those and any other less significant reasons which may have been present, there was a larger motivation. I had an assumed need to prove that even someone as messed up as me could do better than my father. It wasn't a true need. We should never need to find our identity or worth in comparison or contrast to another. I did not realize at the time that by putting myself in the position of "better", I was trying to justify the fact that I was putting my father in the position of "less". I was putting myself in the position of judge over him, which is something I had been doing my entire life, except this time I was doing so more consciously and purposefully than ever. The temptation to prove myself was greater than any fear of failure in this situation, and so rather than run and hide from the possibility of rejection, I gave in to the desire to be looked upon as better. Better than the father who had run out on this precious little girl, and most certainly better than the so-called father who had abandoned me.

I never once asked to be called "dad", "daddy", nor any variation thereof. Not with my words, but I tried to earn it with my actions. Even though my motive was somewhat selfish, I started to make some positive changes. Acknowledging that my earnings could improve so that I could better provide, I enrolled in evening courses at the local college to work toward my first degree. I would say Friday nights at the bar became nothing but a memory if I'd had memories of them to begin with. My time was spent on work, school, and my girls. As for that other matter of feeling like I always had to look over my shoulder just in case the real father decided to show up one day, that slowly faded over time. The closer we became, the further that fear was from my mind. Eventually, I was given what seemed to be the epitome of assurance when Marianne said *"yes"* and allowed me to slip the ring for which I had saved for months on her finger. Considering this commitment, it only made sense to sign a lease on an apartment where the three of us could live together. My mother was so pleased at the independence I had found that as I was packing up for this move, she came to the point of hurling a Scrabble game down the basement stairs. Although she never outright said anything negative about Marianne, I believe my mother's intuition about the relationship was upsetting her more than if I had just been striking out on my own. Regardless, her temper was tempered by the notion of having a granddaughter, and so we found peace on that common ground.

Living together made us more of a family unit, as did taking our daughter, as I had come to think of her, to the park or the playground, to one of those places with all of the children's activities and some animal mascot, to the zoo, and various other places. I would happily oblige on any of these outings when LeAnne's little legs became tired and she reached out asking to be carried, especially because it wasn't long before these requests did include "dada!" Being honoured with that title gave me not only a sense of purpose, but of security. I belonged here, I was wanted here, and I felt that nobody could take this away. I was not a usurper nor pretender to this throne; this two-year old girl had crowned me. If you're blessed with someone in your life who looks up to you in the same way, don't take it for granted, and never let it become mundane. It can end without warning.

According to various internet sources which are obviously all true in spite of their discrepancies, an average adult makes either 27 conscious, deliberate decisions each day, or 35,000. Some days, 27 decisions sounds like enough of a formidable feat. I've decided not to even consider the other number. One down, 26 to go. Regardless of how many decisions are made, there are also variations in how decisions are made. We might use logic and reason. We might follow our gut feelings. We might allow our emotions to sway us. Sometimes we just do whatever seems to be easiest; to go with the flow. Everyone else on the highway seems to be exceeding the speed limit, so we decide to keep up regardless of the increased risk. Everyone else in the office is padding the hours they can bill to their clients, so we decide to maximize our margins regardless of integrity. Every other construction company is cutting corners with cheap materials, so we decide to put profits before quality. Every person in our life appears to "...*take up their cross daily and follow [Jesus]*" (Luke 9:23)... or no, wait, they don't, so why should we decide to?

When Satan tried to tempt Jesus, promising to give Him all the kingdoms of the world and their splendor, "*Jesus said to him 'away from me, Satan! For it is written: 'worship the Lord your God, and serve Him only.'*" (Matthew 4:10). Even without direct intervention from Satan, we experience temptation. All of the things of this world are shouting for our attention, trying to usurp our time, our money, our admiration, our adoration. We submit to an ongoing spiral of loving something, giving to it, and loving it more because of what we get back. Some of these things on their own are not bad. It's good to spend time at work or with friends. It's good to use the money we earn to take care of our families. It's good to admire a healthy role model. It's good to adore the ones we love, such as a surrogate daughter or father. Many of the things in this world are good, but all of the things of this world are temporary. When we decide to treasure these things above all else, we're setting ourselves up for heartbreak, *"for where your treasure is, there your heart will be also"* (Matthew 6:21). We're not simply deciding what to do with our resources, we're simultaneously giving our hearts to these things, perpetually propelling ourselves toward inevitable loss and grief.

Jesus encourages us to *"store up for yourselves treasure in heaven, where moths and vermin do not destroy, and where thieves do not break in and steal"* (Matthew 6:20). When I first heard this as a selfish immature Christian, it sounded like a great incentive to do good things and love people; a reason to *"take up my cross daily and follow Jesus"*. I'm logically minded and love deriving outcomes formulaically: do this, get that. I think I may have originally missed the mark on this one. Yes, God is a good father who wants to reward us, but He's much more. Look back at the actual order of Matthew 6:20 – 21. Jesus tells us to store up treasure in heaven not so that we will have treasure, but because then our hearts will be with Him. He wants to protect our hearts. He is seeking us out and has already gone to great lengths to prove His unconditional, unchanging, unending love for us. God is eternal, constant, and available, so every day we can decide 35,000 times whether to accept that love, or to turn from it. We often believe that opening ourselves up and trusting someone automatically introduces the possibility of betrayal, but believing that about God is nothing but transference in action. Transference is basically the idea that if I look a lot like someone who once punched you in the face, you expect me to punch you in the face even though I never have nor would. God will not betray us no matter how much we believe He will. He is grieved when He sees us betray one another and wants to comfort us. Had I known at the time how much comfort could be found in Jesus' arms, I wouldn't have been so completely emotionally destroyed when my treasure was taken from me.

One night, Marianne sat next to me with tears in her eyes, wrapped her arms around my neck, and pressed her forehead to mine. She whispered, "*I don't want to hurt you*", to which I replied, "*then don't*". Don't show me what I should have seen coming. Don't tell me why you haven't been wearing your engagement ring for the past couple of days. Don't explain why Father's day, which was already a tough day for me every year, had recently come and gone as if it were just another Sunday in spite of my apparently unreasonable hopes. Don't tell me you don't want me anymore. Don't pack your things and move out. Don't take your love away. Don't take LeAnne's love away. Don't make me feel worthless. Don't abandon me. Don't leave me in a state where walking home from work one day I would pause in the center of a bridge and be enticed to end my current state within the current of the rushing river beneath. Don't... just, don't. In spite of all we had shared, in spite of my objections, in spite of me, Marianne had made her decision.

Many of us know the feeling of a partner deciding to leave us. Some of us know the feeling of having a child taken away. LeAnne made no decision to sever her relationship with me, that decision was made for us. She was young enough that she may have no memory of our time together, but I remember. I remember reading her stories at bedtime. I remember how pleased she was at my mediocre job of putting her hair in pigtails. I remember the squeals of joy when she first started pedalling around on the tricycle I unveiled at her third birthday. I remember the ecstatic look on her face the day I came home with a cardboard box, placed it in front of her, and a kitten popped out. I don't seem to remember the tantrums, the spilled milk, or the disgusting diapers even though I'm sure those things were all present at times. I loved the daughter I had, and therefore chose to set the good times to memory and to cast the less pleasant moments to the wind; eventually.

In 1 Peter 4:8 we read "*above all, love each other deeply, because love covers over a multitude of sins*". The love we have for children can cover over the things that really don't matter in the end, in the same way that God, our Father's love for us is gracious, kind and forgiving. Nothing can separate us from His love (see Romans 8:38-39), nothing can take us away from Him in the way a daughter was removed from my life. His love is always there, always available for those who would just believe and decide to accept it. I imagine that the pain and grief I experienced must have paled in comparison to God's when we make an active decision to ignore His love, to ignore Him, even if He tries to get our attention 35,000 times in one day. Yet, even in the deepest sorrow I had experienced up to that time, I continued to make that decision. At the time, this was where desperation met aimlessness and hope seemed to have been lost.

Not That Cliché About Onions

"You may not control all the events that happen to you, but you can decide not to be reduced by them." – Maya Angelou

In his *"Ode on a Distant Prospect of Eton College"*, the English poet Thomas Gray coined the phrase *"Ignorance is bliss"*. This idiom may be true to some extent. For example, when choosing to eat a hamburger from certain fast-food restaurants, you may not be pleased to have the taste experience ruined by the knowledge of the actual contents of the so-called beef patty. In more significant matters, I disagree and would personally advocate for knowledge. It might hurt initially to find out if a friend has been gossiping behind your back, if your partner has been cheating, or if your own son has been stealing money from you. Whether your reaction to these kinds of situations is to place boundaries on the relationship, end the relationship altogether, or to find mutual agreement for restoration, it is mature and healthy to accept short term pain as a necessary conduit toward long term wholeness. You may have also heard that *"what you don't know can't hurt you"*. Again, I must disagree. Even in the case of certain fast-food hamburgers, enjoyment can turn to consequence after only a few short hours. Ignoring the impacts of our hand-me-down behaviours and attitudes in favour of following the seemingly easier path may not always lead to such immediate consequence, but will lead to consequence nonetheless.

I once went through minor surgery to remove a basal cell carcinoma from my right cheek. That is, the one on my face. This was a relatively insignificant form of skin cancer which posed no actual threat unless left unchecked for years, or even decades. Regardless of the length of time it would have taken to grow, the smart decision was to opt for removal. I'm quite thankful for the advent of local anesthetic. It certainly didn't feel pleasant to have a needle stuck in my face multiple times around the site of the impending surgery, but without the freezing, the pain of a knife cutting into my face and scooping out a lump probably would have been more intense. Of course I could have handled such pain, but the doctor insisted on the freezing. Had I tried to ignore the need for the surgery altogether, the cancer would have grown and the eventual removal would have been inevitable. I may not be a surgeon, but I think it's safe to assume that removing a larger tumor would require more cutting. I would also assume that more cutting has the potential for more pain. Had I never asked my doctor his opinion of the suspicious bump on my face, I would not have known that it required removal. I would not have had a needle repeatedly stuck into my face. Yet, a day would have come when my neglect to consistently apply sunscreen or to wear a hat would have eventually caused me much greater pain than the equivalent of a few pin-pricks.

The removal of the cancerous lump was complete in one round. The process, referred to as Mohs surgery, entails on-site analysis of the removed skin while the patient waits with nothing but some gauze taped over the open wound. If the cancer has spread to the full depth of the layer which was removed, then another layer is removed. This is repeated until the inner part of a layer tests as cancer free. The process can be similar to remove the symptoms of abandonment, of abuse, or other traumatic experiences. We may need to remove our tendency to push others away before they hurt us first. Then, as we begin to experience relationships, we may discover that the symptoms of our trauma go deeper. We need to work on our fear of being alone, and the anxiety and fear of saying the wrong thing to someone, that thing that will make them want to discard our relationship. Layer after layer of cancerous tendencies need to be removed until none remain. Also, in the same way that I am now expected to visit the dermatology specialist every six months for a check-up, we need to consistently examine whether our negative tendencies are beginning to re-emerge. Furthermore, just as the dermatologist checks not only the site of the initial tumor, we must understand that our behavioural cancers can metastasize in new areas.

We need to know that what we don't know can hurt us. We also need to know that the symptoms of our mental, emotional, and spiritual ailments can hurt other people. We are not responsible for other people's thoughts, feelings, or reactions, but we are responsible to control the things to which we give them opportunity to react. I cannot control whether a person's eyes shift to my cheek during a conversation, but rather than a malicious looking lump on my face being the reason, I prefer the scar. Rather than the potential conversation about what might be wrong with me, I can now tell a story about something that I have overcome. It's not a tumor, it's a testament.

Acknowledging that my fatherlessness and subsequent feelings of abandonment and worthlessness were causing issues in my life was a painful experience, especially as I began to poke at those old wounds in the same way a doctor might examine a bone that has broken and healed incorrectly. A friend of mine once fractured both of her wrists in a rollerblading accident. Living in a country without government-funded healthcare and lacking insurance at the time, she and her sister wrapped and set her wrists to the best of their ability. Over the course of months and then years, a nagging ache worsened to a chronic pain because of the minimal "good enough" attention initially given to the problem. Now living in Canada and easily able to afford the free healthcare, my friend visited a doctor who recommended that her wrists be re-broken (in a controlled setting) and professionally set so they could mend properly. Thinking that a medical professional, an individual who has taken an oath to do no harm, would recommend and perform this procedure tells me that leaving ourselves in a state of deterioration is even more harmful. It is sometimes worse to continue on partially healed than it is to re-inflict the original wound. Sometimes, we need professional help to do this, especially for mental and emotional trauma which we ourselves are not ready nor equipped to address alone. Sometimes, there are things we can examine on our own if they're the emotional equivalent of breaking open a layer of skin to remove a splinter. Sometimes, it might be best to go through multiple rounds, removing one layer of cancerous characteristics at a time. Most times, we need not only an outside source to help us conclude that healing is necessary, but also motivation to go through the short term pain which leads to the long term gain. I never expected a gift which initially seemed like a subtle ultimatum to turn out to be the catalyst for my healing.

That Wednesday was not a birthday, an anniversary, or of any particular significance to either of us, but when I got to her apartment after work that day Lori presented me with one of those gift bags stuffed with crepe paper and some mystery object. She has always been a generous person, and after seven months of knowing this about her the layer of suspicion through which I previously would have viewed this act was nowhere in sight. Still, I could tell there was something special about this gift from the way Lori seemed more nervous than normal about how I would receive it. As I reached into the bag and pulled out the bible, an extra thick one with notes at the bottom of every page to explain many of the verses, she began to explain. "*I might want to start going to church again, and I think it's something we could do together*". By this time, I had become wise enough to know that "*might*" meant "*do*" and that "*could*" meant "*should*" in this particular case. I knew that Lori would have called herself a Christian, and that her parents most certainly did. She had been raised with church at least every Sunday and sometimes more often, and had even attended a bible college after graduating high school. She never seemed to be the kind of person that secular culture makes Christians out to be though. Maybe the difference in spirit that I could already sense from her enticed me into acceptance of this gentle ultimatum. Maybe the fact that it was September 12th, 2001, and the world had just changed forever played some role. One thing that was certain was my world would never be the same.

For a time after Marianne had left, I was running on empty yet still running away. Running away from my thoughts, my feelings, and the truth. I had no direction, no plan, and if there was any hope for my future, it was not in my own heart. I would fill my time with work, school, work, school, the bar, rinse, repeat. Even then, or perhaps it is more appropriate to say especially then, God was pursuing me. One day I hopped on the city bus and headed straight for the bench at the very rear where the rebels like me sit. As I was just getting comfortable, some random young man asked, "*can I tell you my testimony?*" I didn't know what he meant. Maybe he was rehearsing for a court date. Setting aside the headphones which I had nearly donned prior to this interruption, I begrudgingly muttered "*sure, why not?*" and with a huge grin he proceeded to tell the story of the time he was electrocuted. I don't recall all of the details; I likely wasn't paying enough attention to commit the story to memory to begin with. What I do recall is that he was not trying to establish grounds for a lawsuit against the perpetrator of his accident, he was actually trying to present evidence for the existence and intervention of God. Apparently, the shock he received was more than lethal. He should have died, yet here he was, proclaiming that Jesus Himself had taken his hand at that exact moment and held it until the time he awoke to the sound of his mother praying at the side of his hospital bed. When he asked if he could pray for me, I told him we had reached my stop. I got off the bus, and waited for the next one to take me the rest of the way to my actual destination, ironically thinking, *"please God, no crazies on the next bus"*.

Sometimes as you run, you notice a stone in your shoe. A tiny pebble that isn't worth stopping to remove, but large enough that you know with every stride that it is there. That young man's story nagged at me in the same way. The idea that God cared enough to step off of His throne and personally intervene in a person's life kept resurfacing in my mind, regardless of how many times I would quell it with the *"but not for me"* rebuttal. In spite of how stubborn I was in my assertion that I was special enough to be forsaken, just like a stone might break the skin of your foot when you step on it enough times this truth of God's love broke through a layer of unbelief which had surrounded my hardened heart. A seed had been planted in the deep, dark soil of my soul.

As I continued to learn how to live alone for the first time in my life, I also distanced myself from the social circle into which I had previously imposed myself; that of Big Brother and the pack where he belonged. Paying for school, rent and other bills on my own left less funds for the weekly trips to the bar, and I certainly wasn't eager to revisit the place where Marianne and I had met, lest that mistake be repeated. As tempting as it was, I didn't completely isolate myself. I was paying my way through college and keeping up with the bills by working as a telemarketer, which opens up the age old debate *"does the end justify the means?"* I assure you I have repented of my wrong, but I also assure you I came away with firsthand experience of the truth that *"we know that in all things God works for the good of those who love Him, who have been called according to His purpose."* (Romans 8:28). You might say I didn't even know God at the time, let alone love Him, but I believe that because God is outside of time, He can and does work retroactively in our lives. He orchestrated events such that a co-worker would become the best friend I've ever had.

There was a group of us who would spend our breaks together on a coffee run, in the alley out back smoking, or in the food court of a nearby mall for lunch. There would be the occasional outing outside of a work setting to celebrate a birthday or other event, and I was content with that level of social interaction, but God had other plans. *"He who began a good work in you will carry it on to completion until the day of Christ Jesus."* (Philippians 1:6), and so the seed in my heart needed watering. For some reason, Jude took a liking to me and began to invite me to spend time together without the group. We became friends rather quickly, bonding over our eerily similar stories. His father had also committed a vile act when Jude was a young child. He had dealt with many of the same struggles and questions as I. As if that wasn't enough, he had also been recently dumped by a single mother, also named Marianne; not the same one, but what are the odds? As we became closer and Jude accepted me for who I was, a layer of defensiveness peeled away. Jude was another Christian who didn't fit the cultural stereotype; it was okay for us to drink a couple of beers once in a while, he let me see that he got angry sometimes, he was able to admit that he wasn't perfect. Jude would talk about his faith as a journey toward who he was meant to be rather than portray the false persona of who people might have expected him to be.

When I later became more familiar with the stories within the bible, I began to use the term "Moses moment". One day while out in the desert just doing his thing, Moses noticed a bush which was on fire but did not seem to burn up. He went over to investigate, and his entire future changed as a result. One day Jude told me about his Moses moment; a time when he was angry with God and tired of going through the motions. The details of the story are his to tell, but suffice it to say that when Jude bared his heart and soul before God, God showed up in a way that could only have been Him. Hearing about this experience, another example of God personally intervening in a person's life, subtle cracks began to form on another layer of my defenses. Again, I tried to patch the holes with the same old *"but not for me"* rebuttal, but this wasn't some random guy on the city bus where all kinds of strange folk are found. This was an intelligent, wise, rational person with whom I had a relationship and for whom I had a high level of respect. This was someone I knew well enough to refer to as my best friend. This was more real, more trustworthy. If I wanted to deny God's existence or His desire to father us I would have to call Jude either crazy or a liar, which I knew he was not. Like bubble-gum on a leaky pipe, my pitiful attempts to continue transferring my feelings and assumptions about my biological father onto God began to stretch beyond capacity and fail. Water began to flow through to the seed within, making me more receptive to the gift I would soon receive.

Jude was the first to notice that I had noticed Lori for more than her supervisory skills. Although she wasn't my direct supervisor, I was reluctant to test the boundaries our HR department would undoubtedly try to enforce if they caught wind of any attempts at pursuit I might make. As good a man as he is though, Jude was never overly fond of rules. He encouraged me to see where things might lead, and found a way to motivate me past my reluctance to make my heart vulnerable once again. He told me the story of the summer he had worked on a ranch despite his lack of experience. His duties didn't involve actually riding a horse, but as time went on and his confidence grew there came a time when he just had to try. It may have been more cockiness than confidence, and it may have had something to do with the more experienced men at the ranch goading him on, but either way Jude saddled a horse, mounted up, and was soon thrown to the ground. He thought he had learned his lesson, but there was one yet to come. As Jude began to lead the horse back to the stable, his boss stopped him and said, *"son, the best thing you can do when that happens is to get right back on the horse, because if you wait, you never will"*.

This time, with some instruction and guidance, Jude rode successfully. At the end of it, his boss gave him a belt buckle and a decree: *"you can have this on two conditions. First, every time you look at it you remember that your present failures are not a guarantee of future failures. Always get back on the horse. Second, when the time comes, and you'll know it when it does, you pass this buckle along to someone who needs to hear the same thing"*. As he finished telling this story, Jude produced that buckle from the pocket of his coat and tore off another layer of my defenses as he repeated those same words to me.

I thank God that I fulfilled my part of the bargain, and that belt buckle is now in the hands of someone I consider a daughter, because the time did come when I knew it was to be passed along, along with its message of redemption. Even the fact that this relationship existed, that after having no biological children of our own Lori and I had this parental relationship with not just one but many was evidence of how God gives good gifts to His children. In her time of metaphorically laying in the mud after being bucked from her horse, I was able to tell this young woman about all God has redeemed in my life and encourage her. I was also able to tell her about the first time I actually wore that buckle to go ride a horse, and how I had literally ended up laying in the mud. Interestingly, I had not been bucked off, but had leaned back and rolled myself off the horse's back as it sprinted toward a fence; even then I knew that sometimes causing yourself *some* pain can prevent a lot of pain. More importantly, I was able to convey the story of metaphorically getting back on the horse to this young woman; a story which she could clearly see had a happy ending, inspiring her on toward her own.

Back in that telemarketing firm where Jude and I worked, we received word that a client known for easy sales was bringing in some work and there would be an opportunity for a limited number of us to join the team. My co-workers and I began jockeying for position. The competition to be chosen took shape not only in measurable work-related key performance indicators, but also in underhanded tactics. I'm not advocating for cheating nor for bribery, but I am glad that sometimes, it works. Lori happened to be the lead for this particular sales campaign, and we had happened to have just recently expressed our mutual disdain for the upcoming made-up, over-commercialized holiday, Valentine's Day, which also happened to be the launch date for this campaign. I suggested that if I were on her team, Lori might find a valentine on her desk that day. I thank God that once again that I fulfilled my part of the bargain.

No HR department on Earth with whatever rules they tried to enforce could have kept us apart from then on. Ours tried and failed. When given the two options of either breaking up or being fired, I chose option three and quit. They say, "*when you know, you know*", and even though I'd thought so before, I hadn't truly known what knowing was. There were no defenses nor pretenses between us in spite of the baggage each of us carried. Neither of us wanted the other to become the person we wanted; we simply wanted one another. The people we were to the world would be left at the door, and we loved one another for who we were rather than who we portrayed ourselves to be. Lori saw past the layers of hurt, shame, and guilt I had built up over my lifetime, and I welcomed her in. Back in the days of pay-as-you-go cell phone plans, a $200 phone call was a small price to pay for the pleasure of talking long into the night. Yes, one call, not the entire monthly bill. Meeting for morning coffee dates before the workday became routine. Weekends together became something to be taken for granted. I've heard it said that people don't want to be "taken for granted", but I was glad to be. It is absolutely "granted", a given and a guarantee, that she comes before any other people or plans. I love that Lori could, and still can always count on me to be available to her, to make her my priority.

Even when, seven months into our relationship, Lori's gift presented me with the choice of either confronting the fear of change so that we could grow together or staying comfortable in what was actually my emotional deathbed, I chose life and love. I may not have known at the time that I was choosing so much more, but I knew that I was choosing to continue our relationship. It turned out that by choosing to accept Lori's gift, I was accepting another gift from God. I chose to leave my dark, dank cave in favour of the sunlight, to confront the image in the funhouse mirror. I accepted the invitation into wholeness, knowing I was not just a tag-along, but that my presence was wanted. I chose to turn off the auto-pilot, to correct course. I chose to try, even though trying could be hard. I chose to accept that I would need help from others to learn the way to redemption. These were not all conscious thoughts, let alone conscious decisions. Only in retrospect do I see that one choice meant so much. I simply chose to read, with an open mind.

As recommended to me, and as I would now recommend to others, I started reading in the New Testament. I had previously heard the general overview of Jesus' birth and of His death due to their resultant holidays, but the events in between were new to me. I must admit, it seemed a tad unfair when I read *"a voice from heaven said, "this is my Son, whom I love; with him I am well pleased"'* (Matthew 3:17). Jesus already had a dad, and now he gets a second? Regardless, I continued on, and I began to like this guy. I saw Him stand up to the devil in a face-to-face showdown. I saw Him heal sickness and cast out demons. I heard Him proclaim that the lowly and heartbroken would be seen as worthy. I saw Him spend time with people like me, saying *"it is not the healthy who need a doctor, but the sick"* (Matthew 9:12) when questioned by the social elite about His associations. I saw the way He delivered blunt truth in a way that would convict the people who were full of themselves yet come across as a gentle encouragement to those who were humble and eager for redemption and acceptance. I had come to a point of liking Jesus enough that Lori and I were attending church on a regular basis, though not in a conventional manner.

The large church from a nearby town where Lori's parents attended was interested in planting a new location in our city, and somehow we ended up on the launch team. Lori, I understand; it made perfect sense for her to be in such a position. I had still not used the word "Christian" to describe myself, so your guess is as good as mine as to why I was one of about a dozen people meeting in a basement once a week to plan and strategize and pray for this endeavor. As part of the process, we would attend a Sunday service at various churches in the city each weekend and come away with some ideas about what we would or would not incorporate in our eventual Sunday gatherings. This gave me the opportunity to hear a variety of interpretations and see a range of worship. As I continued to read my bible, as I heard more about Jesus from these different pastors, as I began to see and know more about Him, I began to realize that He saw and knew all of me. Every layer, every pretense, every failure, every lie, every misdeed, every deep dark secret. I fought with all I had to continue on in spite of the resulting feelings of unworthiness to be near to Him. Some weeks, we would attend a church where the sermon left me wanting to give up, but the pain of that layer being scraped off was not the worst pain through which I had ever gone, and so I persisted. Then one week, something just clicked into place.

As they sometimes do at the end of their sermon, one Sunday the pastor of the church we were visiting invited those in attendance to repeat a prayer as he paused after each line so that we could keep pace. The words vary, but the content is similar: asking God for forgiveness, thanking Him that we receive it via Jesus' atoning work, proclaiming a desire to do better, and humbly admitting that we need His presence. I had witnessed this rite a number of times, and now the time had come that I knew I could participate without reservation. It all made sense, and I meant every word. And I lived happily ever after.

Happily Maybe Sometimes After

"No one ever does live happily ever after, but we leave the children to find that out for themselves." – Stephen King, Wolves of the Calla

One spring when I decided it was time to sweep out the garage, I unlocked the door, used my foot to nudge the brick that I had stationed in just the right place to hold the door open, and then hit the button for the overhead door. It wasn't a particularly windy day, certainly not windy enough to blow any more dust in from the driveway. However, the cross breeze must have hit the door in just the right way, with enough force to slam it shut in spite of the brick which was intended to hold it open. Startled by the sudden slam, I instantaneously became incensed at the brick for not doing its job and kicked it, hard. Yes, the brick flew into the wall. Yes, the brick still won that fight. To this day, especially on humid or damp days, the occasional dull ache in the big toe of my right foot serves as a reminder that I need to be vigilant about where I place my anger.

Uncontrolled, misplaced anger is a destructive force which is all too common in those of us who have experienced a perceived injustice, especially if that injustice is a childhood trauma. I realize the fallacy that stereotypes can sometimes be, but traditionally it is a father's role to be the disciplinarian of a family. In absence of a father, a mother can and often does try to fill both roles, but she simply cannot do everything or be everything for her children, often more out of circumstance than through any fault of her own. Her nurturing nature is contradictory to the concept of discipline, therefore it is generally an exception to the norm for us fatherless individuals to experience consistent consequence for our behaviours. A lack of discipline can lead to a child gaining more control than for which they should be responsible. I understand that everyone has a bad day, so if you've ever been that parent in the grocery store with the child throwing a fit to get their way, I'm not judging you. At least, not much. We must realize that if a child learns that throwing a temper tantrum results in getting their way, then the next time they want to get their way, they're going to throw a temper tantrum. As we grow older, our temper tantrums grow into temper tactics. Swearing at someone, slamming a door, cutting off another driver, intentionally pushing someone's buttons, giving the silent treatment, passive aggressive comments, and sarcasm are all examples of how we act out our anger. We might think that we're being subtle, but on the inside we might as well be throwing an absolute fit.

There are numerous opinions on anger management, possibly as many as there are excuses to become angry. Your excuses, those things that you call "reasons", may be different than mine, but they probably all branch out from the same root. If you put some serious thought and effort into actually thinking about the times you've become angry, I'm confident that you will realize you never just become angry. What actually happens is that you experience a situation where you think you do not have control. You then feel fearful about what might happen due to your inability to control the situation. Anger is then the product of your fear, being used as a defense mechanism. Even now as you read these words, because you cannot control my opinion and you experience even the slightest amount of fear that I might be correct, you're probably getting angry at me for saying you're powerless and afraid. Thank you for proving me right.

Anger makes us feel bigger than our fear and bigger than whoever or whatever appears to be controlling the situation. Yet, in truth it makes us smaller than the best version of ourselves. James 1:19-20 says, *"My dear brothers and sisters, take note of this: everyone should be quick to listen, slow to speak and slow to become angry, because human anger does not produce the righteousness that God desires"*. It is interesting that we're encouraged to be *"slow to become angry"*, rather than to not become angry at all. In the context of unity with our community, we read *"In your anger do not sin; do not let the sun go down while you are still angry"* (Ephesians 4:26). This phrasing suggests an assumption that we will become angry, and each of these verses suggests that our responsibility is what we do with that anger. We can allow *"human anger"* to overcome us, and tempt us into the same old fruitless temper tactics. We can hold on to the anger the way we always used to, allowing ourselves to believe the bitterness and blame are good reasons to keep others at arm's length. Then, we can't be abandoned by these people; we've taken control of the situation. Yet somehow, we end up alone anyway, the only difference is it was our decision this time. Take that, dad! I sure showed you who's in control!

Another time when I was driving to Starbucks to meet a friend, I had more than a half an hour to get there on time, and the drive should have taken ten minutes. The route was straightforward; one road where the speed limit was 60 kilometers per hour. Driving the speed limit soon allowed me to catch up to other drivers moving at only 50 kilometers per hour, in every lane. I could feel the anger rising up, regardless of the fact that I would still be early at this speed. How dare people get in my way, driving slower than the posted limit? It's my right to drive 60 kilometers per hour on this road! I took a deep breath, moved to the right-hand lane (signalling the lane-change in spite of my mental state), and at the next opportunity I turned off to a side street, to another route. I knew that this other route meant a speed limit of 50 kilometers per hour. I knew that the detour to a longer route meant I would be at my destination later than I originally would have been. I also knew that the change in perspective, the lower speed limit on this other route being the restriction upon me rather than other people's choices restricting me would calm me. I know how it sounds; it should be reasonable to just accept that I'm behind people who want to drive slower, especially considering there would have been absolutely no harmful outcome. However, I could not accept their alleged control over me, even though I could accept the legal control of the lower speed limit on the other route. Our perspective can sometimes work against us, and might need to change.

Another time, I was not just angry, but filled with indignation when I read the letter that arrived one day in my early twenties. How dare he. Even though the letter was within a letter, sent through a proxy, the mere idea that he could access not just me but send mail to the apartment where I now lived with my wife was a personal violation. This was an affront to the life I had thus far managed to eke out in spite of all the disadvantages he had left me with. That audacious, insolent, selfish piece of trash. That murderer. I probably would have burned that letter on sight if not for Lori's calming presence and good sense to suggest that I wait before deciding whether this was reading material or toilet paper. Deciding not to risk the paper cuts nor setting off the smoke detector, I did read the letter from my father.

"*I'm now living in a minimum security facility*"; you deserve worse.

"*I'll understand if you don't reply*"; postage stamps currently cost $0.43, you're not worth it.

"*I'm sorry for what I've done*"; tell the guy you killed.

"*I don't have much time...I've been diagnosed with a terminal form of bone cancer*"; good. That's GREAT news. I'll be sure to ask my doctor if that might be hereditary at my next check-up. Maybe you'll have finally given me something.

I had no control over his newfound ability to contact me. I had no reason to trust his assertion that this one letter would be his only attempt. I would now have to feel anxious every time I opened the mailbox, and so in retaliation I took control in the only way I knew. I directed my anger back toward Gordon, not openly but by hoping my silence would instill that same anxiety in him. I could have sent a reply which simply said something similar to "forget you", but such a quick stab might put him out of his misery too quickly. I wanted him to wonder if each day might be the day that *I* had found *him* worthy of a relationship. Finally, he would suffer as a result of my choice. I was in control. I had won. That's what holding on to bitterness is, right? Winning?

Some might say I was justified to become angry in the face of what was likely the largest possible trigger to my mental health. I agree to a degree, but staying in that anger was detrimental to my spiritual health. I allowed the one thing I knew about this man to control my decision about how to proceed. He was just some guy in a jail halfway across the country for murdering another man. Based solely on that, there was no reason in my mind to do anything but tear that letter up and move on. I reacted based upon my feelings without considering the facts. That is the biggest regret of my life; I didn't take the time in that situation to consider that a person is not defined by one thing they did one time. If we were, people from my past would be justified to label me useless, unwanted, liar, thief, failure, vandal, hooligan, and more. No single one of those words defines me, nor even describes me at this point in life, yet I was quick to label Gordon "that murderer". I chose to put more importance upon what little I knew about him than on an opportunity to actually know him. Though the concept made sense, I hadn't yet fully understood the difference between knowing about someone and actually knowing them.

"*The Holy Spirit produces this kind of fruit in our lives: love, joy, peace, patience, kindness, goodness, faithfulness, gentleness and self-control.*" (Galatians 5:22 – 23, NLT); nowhere in there is even an implication of anger. Nor do we find any mention of depression, anxiety, despair, sadness, grief, worry, guilt, or many of the other things we feel when we experience a lack of control. I had prayed every line of the prayer verbatim, sure that I caught every word the pastor included. I had every good intention of following through. I had been baptized. I read my bible regularly, I prayed not only to ask, but to listen. Lori and I were attending church every Sunday in spite of the hurts we came away with when the plug was pulled on the church plant we had been part of and the core team drifted apart. We had attended a weekend long "Encounter God" retreat where chains from my past were broken, where I experienced healing and restoration from life-long hurts. If they gave gold stars for attendance, my chart was a galaxy. I knew that I was forgiven for the things I should never have done. I knew I was accepted by God and by the people in our church. I knew Jesus' love was so profound that He would have suffered as He did for even one person, including me. I had times of happiness, but also continued to experience struggles, some of them the same as before any of the changes I had made. I knew so much about God, and yet "happily ever after" remained elusive.

I knew of one thing that was missing, which was to contribute time and talent to the church. After giving as much as we did in the effort at starting a new church only to see it fail, for a time I felt as though I had a spiritual stroke. That side of me was sagging and numb. I was unable to raise my hands in worship. Rather, I was unwilling. I could have forced myself, but the truth is I made a choice to wallow, telling myself I was in a period of rest, recovery, and re-filling. Sometimes we need that recovery period, there is no shame in taking it. Mine just became too comfortable and lasted too long. Then one Sunday as people were filing out, we were nearly at the door when something tugged at my heart and I turned back. Duane, the Associate Pastor was running a Wednesday night bible study, and so I asked if he could use some help with setting up the chairs, making the coffee, and cleaning up after. He was glad to have me come and do so. For a few weeks I did just that, and participated in the group as much as anyone else there. Then one Wednesday after everyone else had left, the cleanup was done, and it was time to lock up, Duane gestured me over to his side at the alarm panel. He handed me a key and said, *"pay attention to the alarm code, you'll need it when I travel back home in a couple of weeks"*. Pastor Duane and his wife Patricia had a vacation planned, and it turned out that volunteer or not, I was going to be leading the bible study the week they were away.

Pastor Duane believed in me when I didn't believe in myself. He saw through the layers of emotional exhaust, of the spiritual stroke, of a somewhat jaded and hardened heart. He saw how I came alive in the group discussions those Wednesday nights and knew I was capable of more. He was right. God has a way of getting us to where He knows we will thrive, we just need to listen when we feel something tug at our hearts. The man I called "Pastor Duane" at that time I now simply call Duane, not out of some diminished respect but out of deeper relationship. Because of his encouragement and mentorship not only in that Wednesday bible study but for a long time to come in a variety of ways and places, I found joy.

Happiness and joy are not the same thing; happiness is a temporary feeling, joy is an ongoing state of being. I found happiness in leading various groups ranging from addiction recovery to financial management. I found joy in seeing the long-lasting growth and well-being of the people who attended those groups, and seeing them grow closer to God. Duane didn't just give me a key and an alarm code, he gave me an opportunity, conduit, and motivation to pay it forward, to *"comfort those in any trouble with the comfort we ourselves receive from God"* (2 Corinthians 1:4). He gave me his confidence. He also gave me an example of many things through his actions: a man who loves God, who does not just love but absolutely treasures his wife, a wonderful father, a man of wise counsel, a strong yet humble spirit, an all-around kind-hearted person. Duane gave me an opportunity to actually know him, and showed a genuine interest in knowing me. Even once that church transitioned to electronic fob-operated locks, I kept that now useless key on my ring with the others where I would see it daily. Even without a lock to fit in, that key is far from useless. In a way, it's an altar to one of the more significant moments God intervened in my life.

When the time eventually came for Duane and Patricia to move back home permanently, the strangest thing happened: I was okay. Of course the news was heartbreaking, and of course I was saddened at the literal distance there would be between us, but our bond would not be broken. Regardless of the nasty little voice in my head which sounds suspiciously like Gollum saying, *"of course! Everyone leaves you!"*, I knew this had nothing to do with me. People make decisions throughout our entire lives which have nothing to do with me, or you. Many of the things that "happen to us" are actually happening in spite of us. They would happen regardless of our presence or even our existence, we're just in proximity to the events or in relationship with the people making the decision. So many of our hurt feelings are due to nothing more than the stories we tell ourselves. I could have chosen to be angry or upset with Duane for leaving me "just like everyone else does", but that would have been ridiculous because he wasn't leaving me. Nor does "everyone else". I maintained joy and regained happiness by spending what time we could together, right up to his final day in the city when I helped load up the moving truck. When everything but the few supplies needed for them to spend one final night in that house was secured away, we sat on the living room floor: Lori and Patricia drinking something fruity, Duane and I sipping whiskey from those all too familiar red plastic cups. Had I been stupid and selfish enough to choose anger over friendship, I would never have been in the position for Duane to say, *"you'll always be just like one of my own kids"*.

Though God had been dropping hints about His existence and His love all throughout my life, and in spite of the knowledge about Him I had finally begun to gather, it was through my relationship with Duane that something more important became obvious. Knowing *about* God is merely an intellectual pursuit. It's a good pursuit, but it is not enough. I had known *about* Gordon, and I live with the regret of never taking the opportunity to know him. I had known *about* Duane before meeting him, and it was a blessing and a privilege to get to know him. I had missed out on one father. I had found a surrogate, a shadow-version of a good father whose kindness and love were mere reflections of God's. I had learned a lot *about* my heavenly Father, I didn't want to stop there and miss out on knowing Him.

Knock Knock. Who's There? I AM.

"Further up, and further in!" – C. S. Lewis, *The Last Battle*
"Here I am! I stand at the door and knock. If anyone hears my voice and opens the door, I will come in and eat with that person, and they with me." (Revelation 3:20)

Turn the tv off. Turn down the volume of the music. I don't care that it's worship music, turn it down and stop singing along. Put your phone down. Better yet, put your phone on silent mode and put it in another room. I don't care that your phone is the device that was playing the worship music, stop arguing with me. If there is someone else with you, either convince them to do the same things, or tell them to leave. Or ask nicely, that may also work. If necessary, be the one to leave the room. After all, Jesus said *"when you go to pray, go into your room, close the door and pray to your Father, who is unseen. Then your Father, who sees what is done in secret, will reward you"* (Matthew 6:6). The point here is that if you want God's attention, a great place to start is by giving Him yours.

If you've spent time in a Christian church, there's a fairly good chance that you've been given similar advice or instruction at some point in time. It isn't bad advice, but God works the way God wants to work regardless of our rites and routines. We try to orchestrate our Moses Moment, thinking that if we do as we're told by the experts, if we play the right songs, if we light the candles or incense, if we wake up early enough, if we pray the right prayer, God will show up personally and powerfully. Do we also believe that with a high school education, we can be granted an interview with the CEO of a multi-billion dollar corporation for a position as a high paid executive? The two are very different in that God is gracious and kind. If we overreach in the business world, we get nowhere. If we overreach with God, He simply gives us what we can handle. "*...God is faithful; he will not let you be tempted beyond what you can bear. But when you are tempted, He will also provide a way out so that you can endure it.*" (1 Corinthians 10:13) Sometimes we're tempted to deepen our relationship with God before we're truly ready to experience more of His glory and majesty. By all means, pursue God! Pray for and watch for your Moses Moment, just don't overlook the steps along the way. I don't know Moses personally so I cannot say for certain, but there may have been a time in his life when he wasn't ready to see a burning bush. He may have freaked out and ran the other way if that had happened at an earlier stage of his maturity.

For some time I pursued my Moses Moment, and became tired. I came to a point where I decided that instead of a Moses-like status, I must be at the level of a one-in-a-million Israelite following along through the desert. Thankfully, I had guidance in my life and was helped to see the truth: Jesus died and resurrected so that we can each have our own personal relationship with Him. Not through a singular prophet, one man who is allowed to climb a mountain and return to the rest of us with a message. Every one of us has the opportunity to hear His voice and open the door, "*everyone who calls on the name of the Lord will be saved*" (Joel 2:32). Not some people, not certain special people. Everyone.

God wants to give every one of us that Moses Moment. Maybe you will get it immediately. Maybe just like me, there could be things you need to stop doing, or start doing before He gives you more. Maybe there is some growth which first needs to take place. We don't get to skip ahead with God; read the story in Matthew 25:14-30 as just one example of what could happen when we do nothing with what God has given us. God might have already said something to you through a sermon, through a wise mentor, or through His word, something which you need to revisit and act upon before He gives you more. Either way, I know that Jesus is alive. I know that He stands at the door and knocks, waiting for us to hear, to let Him in. I know not only because He says so, but from experience.

It wasn't exactly loud in the auditorium, but it wasn't quiet either. Lori and I were at another church event; not a regular Sunday service, but one of those extra things that sometimes happens midweek. A guest pastor had been invited in and was speaking about "listening prayer", the more intricate details of which can be described much better by someone other than me. The important part is that it involves listening (in case you hadn't guessed). We had come to the point of practicing what the pastor had been teaching, and so the approximate one hundred people in attendance had fallen silent. Except, there is always that one loud breather sitting too near, the occasional cough, the rustle of people trying to adjust to a more comfortable position, and of course the incessant whir of the overhead fans. Or was it something other than fans? Was it an actual breeze?

I opened my eyes to see that it was a cool summer's eve as I drove toward the house where I used to live. I had no idea what was compelling me to go there, but the unknown held no unease nor anxiety for me. Instead, I had a strange sense of hopeful expectation. With the car radio off and the windows down, a whispering breeze seemed to mimic a still, small voice urging me ahead to what I would encounter. Had I tried, I never would have imagined anything close to what actually transpired during this visit; the life-altering change which would turn everything around.

I pressed on; rather, the car seemed to move along as if on auto-pilot. Even though I was in the driver's seat and my hands were on the steering wheel, I was exerting no effort at actually navigating my route. As I parked across the street from the three bedroom bungalow and slipped the key out of the ignition, I briefly glanced down at the one key which now unlocked nothing but fond memories of love and encouragement. Before any coherent thought could form, let alone develop into decision, the sight of a man through the picture window of my former home captured my attention. With the sunlight glinting off the pane, I could not make out his features, but it seemed to me that he was watching, waiting for someone.

I wondered if perhaps I was supposed to stand and stride toward the house, but before I could do so much as unbuckle my seatbelt, the figure disappeared from the window and the front door opened. The man stepped out, and I knew immediately and undoubtedly this was Jesus. As He looked directly at me, He simultaneously reached one marred hand back inside the open door, and time seemed to stand still in that moment of anticipation for what would come next.

After what may have been a time, times, or half a time, I watched the five year old boy who I once was step out of that house holding Jesus' hand. They smiled at one another, and then Jesus looked back at me, directly in the eyes. Even though we were thirty yards apart, I clearly heard Him say, *"you don't live here anymore. I am the way home; you belong in my house."*

As the vision faded away, those words permeated my heart and I finally, fully knew my Father's love.

"My Father's house has many rooms; if that were not so, would I have told you that I am going there to prepare a place for you? And if I go and prepare a place for you, I will come back and take you to be with me that you also may be where I am." (John 14:2-3)

About the Author

Sean lives and works near Winnipeg, Manitoba. A strong proponent for mental health awareness, Sean's advocacy transcends the page into an everyday passion for connecting what's logical and meaningful. Known for his masterful interweaving of humour with psychology, Sean's writing both enlightens and makes light of life's hardest conversations with ease.

With a certificate in counselling and experience leading psychoeducational Church programs, Sean works to help guide people toward the reality of their situation today as well as the hope of God for a better tomorrow.

When not working as an Analyst, Sean is spending time with his wife Lori, investing in the lives of their spiritual children, serving their Church family, and enjoying his renewed athleticism on the volleyball court.

Read more at www.unfatherless.com.

www.ingramcontent.com/pod-product-compliance
Lightning Source LLC
LaVergne TN
LVHW041626070426
835507LV00008B/479